The Power of Prayer
and the prayer of power

Clarion Classics

The Christlike Christian, an unknown Christian
The Complete Green Letters, Miles J. Stanford
Fairest Girlhood, Margaret E. Sangster
Fox's Book of Martyrs, W. B. Forbush, editor
The Glory Christian, an unknown Christian
How to Live the Victorious Life,
    an unknown Christian
In His Steps, Charles M. Sheldon
The Kneeling Christian, an unknown Christian
Our Daily Walk, F. B. Meyer
The Power of Prayer, Reuben A. Torrey
The Power of the Blood of Jesus, Andrew Murray
The Prayers of Susanna Wesley, W. L. Doughty,
    editor
Robert Murray McCheyne, A. A. Bonar
The Spirit of Prayer, Hannah More
They Found the Secret, V. Raymond Edman
With Christ in the School of Prayer, Andrew Murray

The Power of Prayer

and the prayer of power

R.A. Torrey

CLARION CLASSICS
Zondervan Publishing House
Grand Rapids, Michigan

THE POWER OF PRAYER
Copyright © 1924 by Fleming H. Revell Company

Formerly published under the title:
The Power of Prayer and the Prayer of Power

Zondervan Books Edition 1971

Library of Congress Catalog Card Number 74-156243

Clarion Classics are published by Zondervan
Publishing House, 1415 Lake Drive, S.E.,
Grand Rapids, Michigan 49506

ISBN 0-310-33311-3

Printed in the United States of America

89   90   91   92   93 / AK / 34   33   32   31   30

Contents

INTRODUCTION

The great need of the church, today, and of human society as a whole, is a genuine, God-sent revival. It is either revival or revolution, and a revolution that will plunge human society and civilization into chaos and utter confusion. It is a time of wide-spread apostasy. This may be the last apostasy from which we will be saved by the return of our Lord Jesus to this earth to take the reins of government into His own thoroughly competent hands. That would, of course, be the greatest and most glorious of all revivals, and a revival that would never end.

But we do not know that this *is* the final apostasy. There have been more thoroughgoing and appalling apostasies in the past than this one is at the present hour. The apostasy in England in the time of the Wesleys, and in America at the time of Jonathan Edwards, was far more complete than the present apostasy is. The apostasy in this country at the opening of the nineteenth century was far more appalling, at least as regards university life, than the apostasy of today. It was the revival under the Wesleys and their associates that saved the church and saved civilization in their day. Even so thoroughgoing a rationalist as Lecky, the historian, admits that it was the revival under the Wesleys that saved civilization in England. And it was the Great Awakening under the leadership of Jonathan Edwards and others that saved the church in America.

Our sorest need today is a deep, thoroughgoing, Spirit-wrought, God-sent revival. Such revivals as far as man's agency is concerned always come in one way— by prayer. It was Jonathan Edwards' Call to Prayer that brought the Great Awakening. The wondrous revival of 1857 was brought by city missionary Landfear's stirring the Christians of New York City to prayer. It was the prayer of the four humble Christians of Kells, and the prayers of others, that brought the marvelous Ulster revival of 1859-'60.

The writer of this present book, at the request of D. L. Moody, late in the nineteenth century wrote a book entitled *How to Pray*; and God used that book to stir many thousands to pray; and the great work in Australia and New Zealand in 1902, extending over to England, Scotland, Ireland, and Wales (the great Welsh revival of 1904) and to India and many lands, resulting in the conversion of hundreds of thousands of souls, was the direct outcome of the publication of that book.

The present book is much fuller and more complete than *How to Pray,* and covers the whole subject of prayer, not only in its relation to revivals, but in its relation to the various departments of Christian life and activity. The chapters are composed largely of addresses on prayer that the writer has given as he has gone around the world, preaching the Gospel. They have grown through the twenty-two years and more that he has been engaged in this work. In their present completed form they were delivered to his own people in the Church of the Open Door, Los Angeles, and they were broadcast over the radio to perhaps 100,000 people (some say far more) each week in places from one mile to 3,000 miles away. These were "listening in" Sunday after Sunday, in the autumn and winter and spring of 1923 and 1924.

As the author writes this preface he is in the midst of a revival in Winnipeg, Canada, where last night 5,000 people crowded into a rink that only seats 4,100, and many were unable to get in. Many men, women and children made a public confession of having accepted Christ in that hour. Shall we have a revival of great power extending over many lands? I believe we shall. God grant that this book may hasten it!

R. A. TORREY

INTRODUCTION TO 1955 EDITION

In Morehead, Kentucky we used this book for background reading in my church—with special thought given to its suitability as a *text* for the prayer meeting. For about six months we had not had a prayer meeting. Then one Sunday morning one of our Bible classes had a time of prayer. Afterward their teacher approached me and said, "We feel as if we should have a prayer meeting!" That was the beginning.

The six copies of this book which I had were passed from person to person throughout the church.

About two years later we had a revival meeting— Dr. Virgil L. Moore, now gone to be with the Lord, was the preacher and Rev. Wilbur Wilson was the song leader. The city of Morehead also houses the State Teachers College. During our revival meeting it was estimated that some 275 persons were saved or consecrated their lives. Dr. Moore said of it, "If a preacher has one like this in a lifetime, there will not be another!" He was referring to my ministry. I reminded him, however, that "God's grace is always the same. He is the same and when we are the same in Him then we can expect great things." I witnessed many revivals after that.

I hasten to point out that there was nothing offensive in that revival. It was a silent, powerful movement of the Spirit of God. Our church took into its fellowship eighty members the closing Sunday morning and evening. Other churches in the city added a great many members to their fellowship.

One morning, Dean William H. Vaughan of Morehead State Teachers College, introduced me as the chapel speaker and said, "I had about come to believe that there was not much to the church, but our speaker this morning has changed that impression. Since he came to our city, his church has expanded its ministry to such an extent that every other church in Morehead has benefited."

I firmly believe that this book, *The Power of Prayer*, is the greatest book I have ever read on prayer during my thirty-two years in the ministry.

—ALBERT R. PERKINS
Centenary Methodist Church

Danville, Kentucky

The Power of Prayer
and the prayer of power

1

THE POWER OF PRAYER

"Ye have not, because ye ask not."—JAMES 4:2.

A message from God is contained in those seven short words. Six of the seven are monosyllables, and the remaining word has but two syllables and is one of the most familiar and most easily understood words in the English language. Yet there is so much in these seven short, simple words that they have transformed many a life and brought many an inefficient worker into a place of great power.

You will find these seven words in James 4:2, the seven closing words of the verse, "Ye have not, *because ye ask not.*"

These seven words contain the secret of the poverty and powerlessness of the average Christian, of the average minister, and of the average church. "Why is it," many a Christian is asking, "that I make such poor progress in my Christian life? Why do I have so little victory over sin? Why do I win so few souls to Christ? Why do I grow so slowly into the likeness of my Lord and Savior Jesus Christ?" And God answers in the words of our text—"Neglect of prayer. You have not, because you ask not."

"Why is it," many a minister is asking, "that I see so little fruit from my ministry? Why are there so few conversions? Why does my church grow so slowly? Why are the members of my church so little helped by my ministry, and built up so little in Christian knowledge and life?" And again God replies: "Neglect of prayer. You have not, *because you ask not.*"

13

"Why is it," both ministers and churches are asking, "that the church of Jesus Christ is making such slow progress in the world today? Why does it make so little headway against sin, against unbelief, against error in all its forms? Why does it have so little victory over the world, the flesh, and the devil? Why is the average church member living on such a low plane of Christian living? Why does the Lord Jesus Christ get so little honor from the state of the church today?" And, again, God replies: "Neglect of prayer. *You have not, because you ask not.*"

When we read the only inspired church history that was ever written, the history of the early church as it is recorded by Luke (under the inspiration of the Holy Spirit) in the *Acts of the Apostles,* what do we find? We find a story of constant victory, a story of perpetual progress. We read, for example, such statements as this in Acts 2:47, "The Lord added to the church *daily* those that were being saved"; and such statements as this in Acts 4:4, "Many of them which heard the Word believed; and *the number of the men came to be about five thousand";* and such statements as this in Acts 5:14, "And believers were the more added to the Lord, *multitudes* both of men and women."

And such statements as this in Acts 6:7, "And the Word of God increased; and the number of the disciples *multiplied* in Jerusalem exceedingly; and *a great company of the priests were obedient to the faith."*

So we can go on, chapter after chapter, through the book, and in every one of the twenty-seven chapters after the first we find the same note of victory. I once went through the *Acts of the Apostles* marking the notes of victory, and without one single exception the triumphant shout of victory rang out in every chapter. How different the history of the church as here recorded is from the history of the church of Jesus Christ today. Take for example, that first statement, "The Lord added to the church daily (that is every day, or, as the Revised Version puts it, 'day by day') *those that were being saved."* Why, today if we have a revival once a year with an accession of fifty or sixty members and spend all the rest of the year slipping back to where we were before, we think we are doing pretty

14

well. But in those days there was a revival all the time and accessions every day of those who not only "hit the trail" but were (really) "being saved."

Why this difference between the early church and the church of Jesus Christ today? Someone will answer, "Because there is so much opposition today." Ah, but there was opposition in those days; most bitter, most determined, most relentless opposition, opposition in comparison with which that which you and I meet today is but child's play. But the early church went right on beating down all opposition, surmounting every obstacle, conquering every foe, always victorious, right on without a setback from Jerusalem to Rome, in the face of the most firmly entrenched and most mighty heathenism and unbelief. I repeat the question, "Why was it?" If you will turn to the chapters to which I have already referred, you will get your answer.

Turn, for example, to Acts 2:42, "And *they continued stedfastly* in the Apostles' teaching and fellowship, in the breaking of bread and *the prayers.*" That is a very brief but very suggestive picture of the early church. *It was a praying church.* It was a church in which they prayed not merely occasionally, but where they all *"continued stedfastly . . . in the prayers."* They all prayed, not a select few, but the whole membership of the church; and all prayed continuously with stedfast determination. "They *gave themselves to prayer,*" as the same Greek word is translated in Acts 6:4. Now turn to 6:4, and you will get the rest of your answer: *"We* will *give ourselves continually to prayer."* That is a picture of the apostolic ministry—it was a praying ministry, and a ministry in which they *"gave themselves continually* to prayer," or, to translate that Greek word as it is translated in the former passage (Acts 2:42), "They continued stedfastly in prayer." *A praying church and a praying ministry!* Ah, such a church and such a ministry can achieve anything that ought to be achieved. It will go steadily on, beating down all opposition, surmounting every obstacle, conquering every foe, just as much today as it did in the days of the apostles.

There is nothing else in the church of today, and the ministry of today, or, to be more explicit, in which you and I have departed more notably and more lamentably from apostolic precedent than in this matter of prayer. We do not live in a praying age. A considerable proportion of the membership of our evangelical churches today do not believe even theoretically in prayer, that is, they do not believe in prayer as bringing anything to pass that would not have come to pass even if they had not prayed. They believe in prayer as having a beneficial "reflex influence," that is, as benefiting the person who prays, a sort of lifting yourself up by your spiritual boot-straps, but as for prayer bringing anything to pass that would not have come to pass if we had not prayed, they do not believe in it and many of them frankly say so, and even some of our "modern ministers" say so.

And with that part of our church membership that does believe in prayer theoretically—and thank God I believe it is still the vast majority in our evangelical churches—even they do not make the use of this mighty instrument that God has put into our hands that one would naturally expect. As I said, we do not live in a praying age. We live in an age of hustle and bustle, of man's efforts and man's determination, of man's confidence in himself and in his own power to achieve things, an age of human organization, and human machinery, and human push, and human scheming, and human achievement; in the things of God this means no real achievement at all. I think it would be perfectly safe to say, that the church of Christ was never in all its history so fully and so skillfully and so thoroughly and so perfectly organized as it is today. Our machinery is wonderful, it is just perfect; but alas it is machinery without power; and when things do not go right, instead of going to the real source of our failure, our neglect to depend upon God and to look to God for power, we look around to see if there is not some new organization we can set up, some new wheel that we can add to our machinery. We have altogether too many wheels already. What we need is not so much some new organization, some new wheel, but "the Spirit of the living creature in the wheels" whom we already possess.

16

Prayer has as much power today, when men and women are themselves on praying ground and meeting the conditions of prevailing prayer, as it has ever had. God has not changed; and His ear is just as quick to hear the voice of real prayer, and His hand is just as long and strong to save, as it ever was. "Behold, the Lord's hand is not shortened, that it cannot save: neither his ear heavy, that it cannot hear." But "our iniquities" may "have separated between us and our God, and our sins" may "have hid his face from us, that he will not hear" (Isa. 59:1, 2). Prayer is the key that unlocks all the storehouses of God's infinite grace and power. All that God is, and all that God has, is at the disposal of prayer. But we must use the key. *Prayer can do anything that God can do, and as God can do anything, prayer is omnipotent.* No one can stand against the man who knows how to pray and who meets all the conditions of prevailing prayer and who really prays. "The Lord God Omnipotent" works for him and works through him.

I. *Prayer Will Promote Our Personal Holiness as Nothing Else Except the Study of the Word of God*

But what specifically, will prayer do? We have been dealing in generalities, let us come down to the definite and specific. The Word of God plainly answers the question.

In the first place, *prayer will promote our personal piety, our individual holiness, our individual growth into the likeness of Our Lord and Savior Jesus Christ as nothing else but the study of the Word of God; and these two things, prayer and study of the Word of God, always go hand-in-hand, for there is no true prayer without study of the Word of God, and there is no true study of the Word of God without prayer.*

Other things being equal, your growth and mine into the likeness of our Lord and Savior Jesus Christ will be in exact proportion to the time and to *the heart* we put into prayer. Please note exactly what I say: "Your growth and mine into the likeness of our Lord and Savior Jesus Christ will be in exact proportion to the

17

time and *to the heart* we put into prayer." I put it in that way because there are many who put a great deal of time into praying but they put so little heart into their praying that they do little actual praying in the long time they spend at it. There are others who may not put so much time into praying but who put so much heart into their praying, that they accomplish vastly more by their praying in a short time than the others accomplish by their praying a long time. God Himself has told us in Jeremiah 29:13: "And ye shall seek me, and find me, *when ye shall search for me with all your heart.*"

We are told in the Word of God in Ephesians 1:3, that God *hath blessed* us with ". . . every spiritual blessing in the heavenly places in Christ." That is to say, Jesus Christ by His atoning death and by His resurrection and ascension to the right hand of the Father, has obtained for every believer in Jesus Christ every possible spiritual blessing. There is no spiritual blessing that any believer enjoys that may not be yours. It belongs to you now; Christ purchased it by His atoning death and God has provided it in Him. It is there for you; but it is your part to claim it, to put out your hand and take it. God's appointed way of claiming blessings, or putting out your hand and appropriating to yourself the blessings that are procured for you by the atoning death of Jesus Christ, is by prayer. Prayer is the hand that takes to ourselves the blessings that God has already provided in His Son.

Go through your Bible and you will find it definitely stated that every conceivable spiritual blessing is obtained by prayer. For example, it is in answer to prayer, as we learn from Psalm 139:23, 24, that God searches us and knows our hearts, tries us and knows our thoughts, brings to light the sin that there is in us and delivers us from it. As we learn from Psalm 19:12, 13, it is in answer to prayer that we are cleansed from secret faults and God keeps us back from presumptuous sins. It is in answer to prayer, as we learn from Psalm 19:14, that "the words of our mouth and the meditations of our heart are made acceptable in God's sight." And it is in answer to prayer, as we learn from

Psalm 25:4, 5, that God shows us His ways and teaches us His path, and guides us in His truth. We also learn from the prayer our Lord Himself taught us, that we are kept from temptation and delivered from the power of the wicked one in answer to prayer (Matt. 6:13 R. V.) As we learn from Luke 11:13 it is in answer to prayer that God gives us His Holy Spirit, and so we might go on through the whole catalog of spiritual blessings and we would find that every one is obtained *by asking for it.* Indeed, our Lord Himself has said in Matthew 7:11: "If ye then, being evil, know how to give good gifts to your children, how much more shall your Father which is in heaven give good things *to them that ask him.*"

One of the most instructive and suggestive passages in the entire Bible, showing the mighty power of prayer to transform us into the likeness of our Lord Jesus Himself, is found in Second Corinthians 3:18, "But we all, with unveiled face beholding as in a mirror [The English Revision reads better, *reflecting as a mirror*] the glory of the Lord, are transformed into the same image from glory to glory, even as from the Lord the Spirit." The thought is this, that the Lord is the Sun, you and I are mirrors, and just as a mischievous boy on a bright sunshiny day will catch the rays of the sun in a piece of broken looking-glass and reflect them into your eyes and mine with almost blinding power, so we as mirrors, when we commune with God, catch the rays of His moral glory and reflect them out upon the world "from glory to glory." That is, each new time we commune with Him we catch something new of His glory and reflect it out upon the world. You remember the story of Moses (not "folk lore" as some would have us believe, but actual history). He went up into the Mount and tarried alone for forty days with God, gazing upon that ineffable glory, and caught so much of the glory in his own face that when he came down from the Mount, though he himself knew it not, his face so shone that he had to draw a veil over it to hide the blinding glory of it from his fellow Israelites. Even so we, going up into the mount of prayer, away from the world, alone with God, and remaining long alone with God, catch the rays of His glory. When we come down to our fellow men it is not so much that our faces shine (though I do believe that sometimes even our faces shine), but our characters, with the glory that we have been beholding. And we reflect out upon the world the moral glory of God from "glory to glory," each new time of communion with Him catching something new of His glory to reflect out upon the world. *Oh, here is the secret of becoming much like God, remaining long alone with God.* If you won't stay long with Him, you won't be much like Him.

One of the most remarkable men in Scotland's history was John Welch, son-in-law of John Knox, the great Scotch reformer. He was not so well known as his famous father-in-law but in some respects he was a far more remarkable man than John Knox himself. Most people have the idea that it was John Knox who prayed: "Give me Scotland or I die." It was not; it was John Welch, his son-in-law. John Welch put it on record before he died, that he counted that day ill-spent that he did not spend seven or eight hours in secret prayer; and when John Welch came to die an old Scotchman who had known him from his boyhood said of John Welch, "John Welch was a type of Christ." Of course that was an inaccurate use of language, but what the old Scotchman meant was, Jesus Christ had stamped the impress of His character upon John Welch. When had Jesus Christ done it? In those seven or eight hours of daily communion with Himself. I do not suppose that God has called many of us, if any of us, to spend seven or eight hours a day in prayer, but I am confident God has called most of us, if not everyone of us, to put more time into prayer than we now do. That is one of the great secrets of holiness; indeed, it is the only way in which we can become really holy and continue holy.

We often used to sing the hymn, *"Take Time to be Holy."* I wish we sang it more in these days. It takes time to be holy; one cannot be holy in a hurry; and much of the time that it takes to be holy must go into secret prayer. Some people express surprise that professing Christians today are so little like their Lord, but when I stop to think how little time the average Chris-

20

tian today puts into secret prayer the thing that astonishes me is, not that we are so little like the Lord, but
that we are as much like the Lord as we are.

II. *Prayer Will Bring the Power of God Into Our Work*

But not only will prayer promote as almost nothing
else our personal holiness, *prayer will also bring the
power of God into our work.* We read in Isaiah 40:31,
"They that wait upon the Lord shall renew their strength;
they shall mount up with wings as eagles; they shall run,
and not be weary; and they shall walk [plod right along
day after day, which is far harder than running or fly-
ing], and not faint."

*It is the privilege of every child of God to have the
power of God in his service.* And the verse just quoted
tells us how to obtain it, and that is by *"waiting upon
the Lord."* Sometimes you will hear people stand up in
a meeting, not so frequently perhaps in these days as in
former days, and say: "I am trying to serve God in my
poor, weak way." Well, if you are trying to serve God
in your poor, weak way, quit it; your duty is to serve
God in *His* strong, triumphant way. But you say I have
no natural ability; then get a supernatural ability. The
religion of Jesus Christ is a supernatural religion from
start to finish, and we should live our lives in supernatural power, the power of God through Jesus Christ,
and we should perform our service with supernatural
power, the power of God ministered by the Holy Spirit
through Jesus Christ. You say, "I have no natural
gifts." Then get supernatural gifts. The Holy Spirit is
promised to every believer that he may obtain the
supernatural gifts which qualify him for the particular
service to which God calls him. "He (the Holy Spirit),
divideth to each one (that is, to each and every believer) severally even as He will" (I Cor. 12:11). It is ours
to have the power of God, if we will only seek it by
prayer, in any and every line of service to which God
calls us.

Are you a mother or a father? Do you wish power
from God to bring your own children up in the "nurture and admonition of the Lord"? God commands you
to do it, and He especially commands the father to do

21

it. God says in Ephesians 6:4: *"Ye fathers,* provoke not your children to wrath: but *bring them up in the nurture and admonition of the Lord."*

Now God never commands the impossible, and as He commands us fathers, and the mothers also, to bring our children up in the nurture and admonition of the Lord it is possible for us to do it. If any one of your children is not saved, the first blame lies at your own door. Paul said to the jailer in Philippi: "Believe on the Lord Jesus Christ, and thou shalt be saved, *and thy house"* (Acts 16:31).

Yes, *it is the solemn duty of every father and mother to lead every one of their children to Jesus.* But we can never accomplish it unless we are much in prayer to God for power to do it. In my first pastorate I had as a member of my church a most excellent Christian woman. She had a little boy of six who was one of the most incorrigible youngsters I have ever known. He was the terror of the community. One Sunday at the close of the morning service his mother came to me and said: "You know ——" (calling her boy by his first name).

"Yes," I replied, "I know him." Everybody in town knew him.

Then she said, "You know he is not a very good boy."

"Yes," I replied, "I know he is not a very good boy." Indeed, that was a decidedly euphemistic way of putting it; in point of fact he was the terror of the neighborhood.

Then his heavy-hearted mother said, "What shall I do?"

I replied: "Have you ever tried prayer?"

"Why," she said, "of course I pray."

"Oh," I said, "that is not what I mean. Have you ever asked God definitely to regenerate your boy and then expected Him to do it?"

"I do not think I have ever been as definite as that."

"Well," I said, "you go right home and be just as definite as that."

She went home, she was just as definite as that; and I think it was from that very day, certainly from that week, that her boy was a transformed boy and grew up into fine young manhood.

22

Oh, mothers and fathers, it is your privilege to lead every one of your children to the Savior. But it costs something to have them saved. It takes much time alone with God, to be much in prayer. It costs also your making those sacrifices, and straightening out those things in your life that are wrong; it costs fulfilling the conditions of prevailing prayer. And if any of you have unsaved children, get alone with God and ask Him to show you what it is in your own life that is responsible for the present condition of your children, and straighten it out at once and then get down alone before God and hold on to Him in earnest prayer for the definite conversion of each one of your children. Do not rest until, by prayer and by your putting forth every effort, you know beyond question that every one of your children is definitely and positively converted and born again.

Are you a Sunday school teacher? Do you wish to see every one of your Sunday school scholars converted? That is primarily your duty as a Sunday school teacher. You are not merely to teach Bible geography and Bible history, or even Bible doctrine, but to get the scholars in your class one and all saved. Do you want power from on high to enable you to save them? Ask God for it.

When my associate, Mr. Alexander, and I were in Sydney, Australia, the meetings were held in the Town Hall which seated about 5,000 people. But the crowds were so great that some days we had to divide the group and have women only in the afternoon, and men only at night. One Sunday afternoon the Sydney town hall was packed with women. I gave the invitation for all who would accept Jesus Christ as their personal Savior, and surrender to Him as their Lord and Master, and begin to confess Him as such before the world, and strive to live from this time on to please Him in every way from day to day. On my left a whole row of young women of, I should say, about twenty years of age, arose to their feet, eighteen in all. As I saw them stand side by side I said to myself, "That is someone's Bible class." Afterwards they came forward with the other women who came to make a public confession of their acceptance of Jesus Christ. When the meeting was over a young lady came to me, her face wreathed in smiles, and she said, "That is my Bible class. I have been praying for their conversion and every one of them has accepted Jesus Christ today."

We were holding meetings in Bristol, England. A prominent manufacturer in Exeter had a Bible class in that city, a class of twenty-two men. He invited all of them to go to Bristol with him and hear me preach. Twenty-one of them consented to go. At that meeting twenty of them accepted Christ. The twenty-first accepted Christ in the train on the way home, and then they all, on their return, gathered around the remaining one who would not go, and he also accepted Christ. That teacher was praying for the conversion of the members of his class and was willing to make the sacrifices necessary to get his prayers answered. What a revival we would have if every Sunday school teacher would go to praying the way he or she ought for the conversion of every scholar in his or her class!

Are you in more public work, a preacher perhaps, or speaking from the public platform? Do you long for power in that work? Ask for it. I shall never forget a scene I witnessed many years ago in the city of Boston. It was at the International Christian Workers' Convention which was held in the old Tremont Temple, seating 3,500 people. It was my privilege to preside at the Convention. On a Saturday morning at eleven o'clock the Tremont Temple was packed to its utmost capacity. Every seat was taken, every inch of standing room where men and women were allowed to stand was taken, and multitudes outside still clamored for admission. The audience was as fine in quality as it was large in numbers. As I looked behind me on the platform, it seemed as if every leading minister and clergyman not only of Boston but of New England was on that platform. In front of me I saw seated the leaders not only in the church life but in the social and commercial and political life of Boston and the surrounding country.

I arose to announce the next speaker on the program; and my heart sank, for the next speaker was a woman. In those days I had a prejudice against any woman speaking in public under any circumstances. But this particular woman was a professing Christian,

and a Presbyterian at that (and I suppose that is orthodox enough for most of us), but she had been what we
call a "worldly Christian," a dancing, card-playing, the-
ater-going Christian. She had, however, had an experience of which I had not heard. One night, sitting in her
beautiful home in New York City (she was a woman of
wealth), she turned to her husband as he sat reading the
evening paper, and said: "Husband, I hear they are
doing a good work down at Jerry McAuley's Mission at
316 Water Street. Let's go down and help them." He
was very much like her: kind-hearted, generous, but
very much of a worldling. He laid aside his paper and
said: "Well, let's go." They put on their wraps and
started for 316 Water Street.

When they arrived they found the Mission Hall full
and took seats back by the door. As they sat and
listened to one after another of those rescued men, they
were filled with new interest. A new world seemed to
open to them; and at last the woman turned to her
husband and whispered: "I guess they will have to help
us instead of our helping them. They've got something
we haven't." And when the invitation was given out
this finely-dressed, cultured gentleman and his wife
went forward and knelt at the altar in the sawdust
along with the drunken "bums" and other outcasts of
Water Street.

But of this I knew nothing. I only knew the type of
woman she had been, and when I saw her name on the
program, as I said, my heart sank and I thought, *What
a waste of a magnificent opportunity; here is this wonderful audience and only this woman to speak to them.*
But I had no authority to change the program; my
business was simply to announce it. Summoning all the
courtesy I could command under the circumstances, I
introduced this lady, and then sank into the chairman's
seat and buried my face in my hands and began to pray
to God to save us from disaster. Some years afterward I
was in the City of Atlanta, and one of the leading
Christian workers of that city, who had been at the
Boston Convention, came to me laughing and said: "I
shall never forget how you introduced Mrs. —— at the
Boston Convention, and then dropped into your chair

and covered your face with your hands as if you had done something you were ashamed of."

Well, I had. But as I said, I began to pray. In a short while I took my face out of my hands and began to watch as well as pray. Every one of those 3500 pairs of eyes were riveted on that woman as she stood there and spoke. Soon I saw tears come into eyes that were unaccustomed to weeping, and I saw men and women taking out their handkerchiefs and at first trying to pretend they were not weeping, and then, throwing all disguise to the winds, I saw them bow their heads on the backs of the seats in front of them and sob as if their hearts would break. Before that wonderful address was over that whole audience was swept by the power of that woman's words as the trees of our forests are sometimes swept by the cyclone.

This was Saturday morning. The following Monday morning Dr. Broadbeck, at that time pastor of the leading Methodist Church in Boston, came to me and said with a choking voice, "Brother Torrey, I could not open my mouth to speak to my own people in my own church yesterday morning without bursting into tears as I thought of that wonderful scene we witnessed here on Saturday morning."

When that wonderful address was over, some of us went to this woman and said to her: "God has wonderfully used you this morning."

"Oh," she replied, "would you like to know the secret of it? Last night as I thought of the great throng that would fill the Tremont Temple this morning, and of my own inexperience in public address, I spent the whole night on my face before God in prayer."

Oh, men and women, if we would spend more nights before God on our faces in prayer, there would be more days of power when we faced our congregations!

2

WHAT DEFINITE AND DESIRABLE RESULTS WILL DEFINITE AND DETERMINED PRAYER PRODUCE?

"The supplication of a righteous man availeth much in its working."—JAMES 5:16 R. V.

"The effectual fervent prayer of a righteous man availeth much" (James 5:16). These words of God set forth prayer as a working force, as a prayer that brings things to pass that would not come to pass if it were not for prayer. This comes out even more clearly in the Revised Version. "The supplication of a righteous man availeth much *in its working.*" While this translation means practically the same thing as the Authorized, it is not only a more accurate translation but it is also a more suggestive one. It tells us that prayer is something that works, and that it availeth much because of its "working." Yes, prayer certainly does work.

A contrast is often drawn by many between praying and working. I knew a man once, an officer in a Sunday school in Brooklyn. One day the superintendent called on him to pray. He arose and said, "I am not a praying Christian, I am a working Christian." But praying *is* working. It is the most effective work that anyone can do; that is, we can often bring more to pass by praying than we can by any other form of effort we might put forth.

Furthermore, prayer, if it be real prayer, the kind of prayer that avails much with God, oftentimes is harder work than any other kind of effort; it takes more out of

27

one than any other kind of effort. When Mr. Alexander and I went to Liverpool for our second series of meetings there, Rev. Musgrave Brown, vicar of one of the leading Church of England parishes in the city, was chairman of our committee. His health gave out the very first week of the meetings and he was ordered to Switzerland by his doctor. Soon after reaching Switzerland he wrote me saying, "I hoped to be of so much help in these meetings and anticipated so much from them, but here I am, way off here in Switzerland, ordered here by my doctor, and now all I can do is to pray." Then he added, "But after all, that is the greatest thing anyone can do, is it not?" Then he added, "And real prayer takes more out of one than anything else, does it not?" Yes, it often does. Real praying is a costly exercise but it pays far more than it costs. It is not easy work but it is the most profitable of all work. We can accomplish more by time and strength put into prayer than we can by putting the same amount of time and strength into anything else.

You will notice that in the Revised Version the word "supplication" is substituted for the word "prayer." The reason for that is this: there are a number of Greek words which are translated "prayer" in the Authorized Version and they have different shades of meaning, sometimes very significant shades of meaning. The Greek word which the Authorized Version translates "prayer" in this passage is a very significant word: *it sets forth prayer as the definite expression of a deeply felt need.* Indeed, the primary meaning of the word is "need." Therefore, our text teaches that, *Definite and determined prayer to God "availeth much."*

The Greek word translated "availeth" is also an expressive and significant word. Its primary meaning is "to be strong," "to have power [or force]," and then "to exercise power." So the thought of our text is that *definite and determined prayer exerts much power in its working,* that it achieves great things. Then in the verses that immediately follow we are told of the astounding things Elijah brought to pass by his prayers, how he shut up heaven for three years and six months so that there was not a drop of rain for that long period; and the Old Testament account tells us that not only was there not a drop of rain, but furthermore, not a drop of dew (I Kings 17:2). When the proper time had come Elijah "prayed again, and the heaven gave rain, and the earth brought forth her fruit." Or, as Mr. Moody used to put it in his graphic way, "Elijah locked up heaven for three years and six months and put the key in his pocket." Now there is no particular need that you or I know of why we should shut up heaven for three years and six months, or, for that matter, for three days; but there is a most imperative need that we bring some other things to pass. There is no other way in which we can bring them to pass than by praying for them, by definite and determined prayer. So we are brought face to face with the tremendously important question: What are some of the definite things that are greatly to be desired at the present time that prayer will bring to pass?

We have already seen two immeasurably important things that prayer will accomplish First, that it will promote our own personal piety, our individual holiness, our individual growth into the likeness of our Lord and Savior Jesus Christ. Second, that it will bring the power of God into our work. Now we will discover from a study of the Bible some other exceedingly important things that the right sort of praying will bring to pass.

I. *Prayer Will Save Others*

Turn to First John 5:16, "If any man see his brother sinning a sin not unto death, he shall ask, and God will give him life for them that sin not unto death."

This is one of the most remarkable statements in the whole Bible on the subject of prayer and its amazing power. The statement of this verse is not only most remarkable, it is also most cheering and most gladdening. God here tells us that prayer will not only bring blessing to the one who prays, but that it will bring the greatest of all blessings, even the blessing of eternal life, to others, to those for whom we pray. It tells us that if we see another sinning a sin not unto death, that is, committing sin, any sin except the one unpardonable sin, we can go to God in prayer for that one and that in answer to our prayer God will give life, eternal life, to this one for whom we have prayed. This passage, of course, is often taken to teach divine healing, and interpreted as if the thought were that the "life" here spoken of was mere natural or physical life, and that by our prayer we could get physical life for one who was sick because of his sinning but who had not sinned the sin which must eventuate in his being removed from this world. But this is not only an incorrect but an impossible interpretation. The apostle John in his writings uses two different Greek words for "life." One signifies physical life, the other signifies spiritual or eternal life; it is never used of natural life, merely physical life. I have looked up every passage where John uses this latter word in his gospel, in his epistles and in the book of Revelation, and not in one single instance does he use the word used in this verse of anything but spiritual or eternal life. This is the word John uses in this passage, and the thought of this passage then is, not that one may obtain physical life, deliverance from natural death, by praying for one who has sinned, but that he can obtain eternal life, salvation in its fullest sense, for the one who has sinned but has not sinned unto death. It is a wonderful thought and a thought full of comfort and encouragement.

We can accomplish more for the salvation of others by praying for them than we can in any other way. I do not mean by this that when we feel our responsibility for the salvation of someone else we should merely pray for them and do nothing else. That is what many do; they are not willing to do their duty and go to them and speak to them about Christ, and so they go to God in prayer and when they have prayed for their salvation they flatter themselves that they have done their whole duty, and thus make their prayer an excuse for their cowardice and laziness and neglect of duty. That kind of praying is a mockery; it is simply an attempt to cover up and excuse our neglect of duty; and God will pay no attention whatever to prayers of that sort. God never gave us the wonderful privilege of prayer as a make-shift to cover up our laziness and neglect of duty. But, if we are willing that God should use us in answering our own prayers, willing to do anything that God may guide us to do to secure the salvation of those for whom we are praying, willing to do anything in our power to bring about the salvation of those for whom we pray, then we can accomplish far more for their salvation by praying for them than in any other way.

Did you ever think how our Lord Jesus Himself accomplished things by praying that even He could not accomplish in any other way? Take for example the case of Simon Peter. He was full of self-confidence and therefore was in imminent danger. Our Lord endeavored by His teachings and by His warnings to deliver Peter from his self-confidence. He told Peter definitely of his coming temptation and of his fall, but Peter, filled with self-confidence, replied: "If all shall be offended in thee, I will never be offended" (Matt. 26:33). And again, "I will lay down my life for thee" (John 13:37). Teaching failed, warning failed, and then our Lord took to prayer. He said, "Simon, Simon, behold, Satan asked to have you, that he might sift you as wheat: but *I made supplication for thee,* that thy faith fail not; and do thou when once thou hast turned again, establish thy brethren" (Luke 22:31, 32). Satan got what he asked— he had Simon in his sieve and sifted him; and, oh, how poor Simon was battered and bruised against the edges of Satan's sieve! But all the time Satan sifted, our Lord Jesus prayed, and Simon was perfectly safe even though he was in Satan's sieve; and all Satan succeeded in doing with him was to sift some of the chaff out of him, and Simon came out of Satan's sieve purer wheat than he ever was before.

It was our Lord's prayer for him that transformed the Simon who denied his Lord three times, and denied Him with oaths and curses, in the courtyard of Annas and Caiaphas, into *Peter, the man of rock,* who faced the very court that sentenced Jesus to death and hurled defiance in their teeth and said, "Ye rulers of the people and elders, if we this day are examined concerning a good deed done to an impotent man, by what means this man is made whole; be it known unto you all, and to all the people of Israel, that *in the name of Jesus Christ of Nazareth, whom ye crucified,* whom God raised from the dead, even in him doth this man stand here before you whole" (Acts 4:8-10).

Prayer will reach down, down, down into the deepest depths of sin and ruin and take hold of men and women who seem lost beyond all possibility or hope of redemption, and lift them up, up, up until they are fit for a place beside the Son of God upon the throne.

Many years ago in Chicago, in the early days of Mr. Moody's work in that city, there was a desperate man who used to attend the meetings and try to disturb them. He was a Scotchman and had been reared in a Christian home by a godly mother, but he had wandered far from the teachings of his childhood. This man was dreaded even by other dissolute men in Chicago. One night he stood outside the old Tabernacle with a pitcher of beer in his hand offering a free drink to everyone that came out of the Tabernacle. At other times he would come into the meetings and into the after-meetings, and try to disturb the workers. One night Major Whittle was dealing with two young men and this desperate Scotchman stood near mocking until Major Whittle turned to the young men and said, "If you set any value upon your souls, I advise you not to have anything to do with that desperate man"; and he only laughed. But his old mother over in Scotland was praying; and one night he went to bed just as wicked and godless as ever, and in answer to his mother's prayer God awakened him in the middle of the night and brought to his mind a text of Scripture that he had forgotten was in the Bible, Romans 4:5. "But to him that worketh not, but believeth on him that justifieth the ungodly, his faith is reckoned for righteousness." That verse of Scripture went home to his heart and he accepted Christ without getting out of bed. He became one of the most active and most useful members of the Moody Church. When I was pastor of the church he was one of the elders, and afterwards became visitor for the church, and he was used of God to lead many to Christ.

Sometime after his own conversion he went to Scotland to visit his old mother. He had a brother in Glasgow in business and this brother was trying to be an agnostic. But the godly mother and converted son prayed for this brother and he was converted and gave himself up to God's work, went to the Free Church

College to prepare for foreign missionary work and for thirty years was a medical missionary in India under the Free Church of Scotland Missionary Board. But there was still another brother, a wanderer on the face of the earth. They did not know where he was, though they supposed he was somewhere on the high seas, but the godly mother and converted brother knelt and prayed for this wandering son and brother. As they prayed that son, unknown to them, was on the deck of a vessel on the other side of the globe, in the Bay of Bengal, not far from Calcutta; and the Spirit of God fell upon that son on the deck of that vessel and he was converted. He was for many years a member of the Moody Church when I was pastor there, and when I went out to Los Angeles he followed me and became a member of our church in Los Angeles, and then died a triumphant death. Prayer had reached half-way round the world and saved instantly a man who seemed utterly beyond hope.

When I was in England holding meetings in the city of Manchester, one of the leading business men came to me and asked me to pray for the conversion of his son. He said, "My son is a graduate of Cambridge University and a brilliant lawyer. He has a wife and two children but he has left them and we do not know where he is. Will you pray for his conversion?" I promised him that I would. Some months afterward this man came to me at the Keswick Convention and said, "I have found my boy. He is in Vancouver, British Columbia. Do you know any minister in Vancouver to whom I could cable?" I told him the name of a friend who was a minister of the Gospel in Vancouver and he cabled him. The next day he came to me and said, "We were too late, the bird has flown, he has left Vancouver. Will you continue to pray for him?" I said I would. At the close of the same year, when we began our second series of meetings in Liverpool, unknown to his father, this son had returned to England and was in Liverpool. He came to our first Sunday afternoon meeting and was one of the first ones to accept Christ. Immediately he began to study for holy orders under the Bishop of Liverpool.

Have you loved ones who are unsaved? There is a

way to reach them: that way is by the throne of God. By the way of the throne of God you can reach out to the uttermost parts of the earth and get hold of your loved ones of whom you have lost all track. God knows where they are and God hears and answers prayer. At the close of the meeting in a certain city a lady came to me and said, "I have a brother above sixty years of age. I have been praying for his salvation for years but I have given up. I will begin again." Within two weeks she came to me and said, "I have heard from my brother and he has accepted Christ."

Yes, yes, yes, "the supplication of a righteous man availeth much in its working," and if we would only pray more and be more sure that we had met the conditions of prevailing prayer, we would see multitudes more of men and women flocking to Jesus Christ. Oh, that we might pray as we ought, as intelligently as we ought, as definitely as we ought, as earnestly and determinedly as we ought, for the salvation of the men, and women and children whom we know are unsaved.

II. *Prayer Will Bring Blessing and Power to Ministers of the Word*

"And take the helmet of salvation, and the sword of the Spirit, which is the Word of God: *with all prayer and supplication* praying at all seasons in the Spirit, *and watching thereunto in all perseverance* and supplication for all the saints, *and on my behalf, that utterance may be given unto me in opening my mouth, to make known with boldness the mystery of the gospel,* for which I am an ambassador in chains; *that in it I may speak boldly, as I ought to speak"* (Eph. 6:17-20 R. V.). Here Paul urgently requests the earnest prayers of the believers in Ephesus for himself, that in answer to their prayers he may preach the Gospel with boldness and with power. Paul made a similar request of every church to which he wrote with one striking exception; that one exception was the church in Galatia. That church was a backsliding church and he did not care to have a backsliding church praying for him. In every other case he urged the church to pray for him. *Here we see the power of prayer to bring blessing and bold-*

ness and efficiency to ministers of the Gospel. A minister may be made a man of power by prayer, and he may be unmade and bereft of power by people failing to pray for him. *Any church may have a mighty man of God for its pastor, if it is willing to pay the price, and that price is not a big salary but great praying.*

Have you a pastor you do not like, a pastor who is perhaps inefficient, or does not clearly know nor preach the truth? Do you want a new minister? I can tell you how to get him. Pray for the one you have till God makes him over.

Many years ago in one of the Cornish parishes of the Church of England, the vicar was not even a converted man. He had but little interest in the real things of God; his interest was largely in restoring old churches and in matters of ritual. There were a great many godly people in that parish and they began to pray to God to convert their minister, and then they would go to church every Sunday and watch for the answer to their prayers. One Lord's Day when he rose to speak he had not uttered many sentences before the people of spiritual discernment realized that their prayers had been answered and a cry arose all over the church, "The parson's converted, the parson's converted!" And it was true. He was not only converted but he was endued with power from on high; and for many years God used that man all over England for the conversion of sinners, for the blessing of all saints, and for the quickening of churches, as almost no other man in the Church of England.

There was a church in the city of Hartford, Connecticut, which had a very brilliant man for its pastor. But the pastor was not sound in doctrine. There were three godly men in that church who realized that their pastor was not preaching the truth. They did not go around among the congregation stirring up dissatisfaction with the pastor, however. They covenanted together to meet every Saturday night to pray long into the night for their minister. So Saturday night after Saturday night they met in earnest and protracted prayer; then Sunday morning they would go to church and sit in their places and watch for an answer to their prayers. One Sunday morning when the minister rose to speak he was just as brilliant and just as gifted as ever, but it soon became evident that God had transformed his ideas and transformed the man, and Dr. Theodore Cuyler is authority for the statement that God sent to the city of Hartford the greatest revival that city ever had, through that minister who was transformed by the prayers of his members. Oh, if we would talk less to one another against our ministers, and more to God in their behalf, we would have far better ministers than we have now.

Have you a minister whom you do like? Do you wish him to be even better, do you wish him to be far more effective than he is today? Pray for him till God gives him new wisdom and clothes him with new power.

Have you ever heard how Dwight L. Moody became a world-wide evangelist? After the great fire in Chicago, Mr. Moody stayed in Chicago long enough to get money together to feed the poor and to provide a new building for his own work, and then he went to England for a rest. He did not intend to preach at all, but to hear some of the great preachers on the other side of the water—Spurgeon, George Müller, and others. He was invited to preach one Sunday in a Congregational church in the north of London, of which a Mr. Lessey was the pastor. He accepted the invitation. Sunday morning as he preached he had great difficulty. As he told the story to me many years afterward, he said, "I had no power, no liberty; it seemed like pulling a heavy train up a steep grade, and as I preached I said to myself, 'What a fool I was to consent to preach. I came here to hear others, and here I am preaching.' As I drew to the close of my sermon I had a sense of relief that I was so near through, and then the thought came to me, 'Well, I've got to do it again tonight.' I tried to get Mr. Lessey to release me from preaching that night, but he would not consent. I went to the evening service with a heavy heart. But I had not been preaching long when it seemed as if the powers of an unseen world had fallen upon that audience. As I drew to the close of my sermon I got courage to draw the net. I asked all that would then and there accept Christ to rise, and about five hundred people arose to their feet. I thought there

36

must be some mistake; so I asked them to sit down, and then I said, 'There will be an after-meeting in the vestry, and if any of you will really accept Christ meet the pastor and me in the vestry.'

"There was a door at each side of the pulpit into the vestry and people began to stream through these doors into the vestry, and I turned to Mr. Lessey and said, 'Mr. Lessey, who are these people?' He replied, 'I do not know.' 'Are they your people?' 'Some of them are.' 'Are they Christians?' 'Not as far as I know.' We went into the vestry and I repeated the invitation in a stronger form, and they all rose again. I still thought that there must be some mistake and asked them to be seated, and repeated the invitation in a still stronger form, and again they all arose. I still thought there must be some mistake and I said to the people, 'I am going to Ireland tomorrow, but your pastor will be here tomorrow night if you really mean what you have said here tonight meet him here.' After I reached Ireland I received a telegram from Mr. Lessey saying, 'Mr. Moody, there were more people out on Monday night than on Sunday night. A revival has broken out in our church and you must come back and help me.' " Mr. Moody hurried back from Dublin to London and held a series of meetings in Mr. Lessey's church that added hundreds of people to the churches of North London, and that was what led to the invitation that took him over to England later for the great work that stirred the whole world.

After Mr. Moody had told me that story I said, "Mr. Moody, someone must have been praying." "Oh," he said, "did I not tell you that? That is the point of the whole story. There were two sisters in that church, one of whom was bedridden; the other one heard me that Sunday morning. She went home and said to her sister, 'Who do you suppose preached for us this morning?' The sister replied, 'I do not know.' Then she said, 'Guess,' and the sister guessed all the men that Mr. Lessey was in the habit of exchanging with, but her sister said 'No.' Then her sister asked, 'Who did preach for us this morning?' And she replied, 'Mr. Moody of Chicago.' No sooner had she said it than her sister turned pale as death and said, 'What! Mr. Moody of

Chicago! I have read of him in an American paper and I have been praying God to send him to London, and to send him to our church. If I had known he was to preach this morning I would have eaten no breakfast, I would have spent the whole morning in fasting and prayer. Now, sister, go out, lock the door, do not let any one come to see me, do not let them send me any dinner; I am going to spend the whole afternoon and evening in fasting and prayer?" And pray she did, and God heard and answered.

God is just as ready to hear and answer you as He was to answer that bedridden saint. To whatever church you belong, and whoever your pastor is, you can make him a man of power. If he is a man of power already, you can make him a man of even greater power.

Will you bear with me while I give you a leaf out of my own experience? When I went to Chicago it was not to take the pastorate of a church but to be Superintendent of the Bible Institute, and of the Chicago Evangelization Society. After I had been there four years the pulpit of the Moody Church became vacant and Mr. Moody and I asked them to call a very gifted preacher from Aberdeen, Scotland; which they did. While we waited to hear from him as to whether he would accept the call, I filled the pulpit; and God so blessed the preaching of His Word that quite a number of the people were praying that the minister from Scotland would not accept the call, and he did not. Then they called me to the pastorate. I could not see how I could take it; my hands were full with the Institute, the lectures, the correspondence and other duties. But Mr. Moody urged me to accept the call; he said, "That is what I have been wanting all the time. If you will only accept the call, I will give you all the help that you ask for, and provide men to help you in the Institute"; and I accepted the call.

The first sermon I preached after taking the pastorate of the church was upon prayer, and in it I said some of the things that I have said here. As I drew toward the close of my sermon I said, "How glad your new pastor would be if he knew that some of you men and women of God sat up late Saturday night, or rose early Sunday

38

morning, to pray for your new pastor"; and many of those dear saints of God took me at my word. Many of them sat up late Saturday night praying for their minister, and many of them rose early Sunday morning to pray for their minister; and God answered prayer. The church building when I took the pastorate would seat 2200 people, 1200 on the first floor and 1000 in the gallery; but in the preceding years only the first floor of the church was filled, and the gallery only opened on special occasions, when Mr. Moody was there or something of that kind. Almost immediately it became necessary to open the gallery; and then in the evening service every inch of standing room would be taken, until we packed 2700 people into that building by actual count, and the police authorities allowed us no longer to let people sit on the stairs or stand in the aisles. Then we had an overflow meeting in the rooms below, which would seat 1100, and oftentimes into the Institute Lecture Hall also.

But that was not the best of it. There were conversions every Sunday; indeed, there were conversions in and about the church practically every day in the week. The great majority of those who were converted did not unite with the Moody Church; they were strangers passing through the city, or people who came from other churches. It came to be quite a custom for some ministers to send their people over to our church to have them converted, then they would go back and join the churches to which they properly belonged. So only a comparatively small proportion of those converted united with our church, and yet the smallest number that we ever received into the church in any one of the eight years I remained there as active pastor was 250. And in those eight years I had the joy of giving the right hand of fellowship to over 2000 new members.

And it went on just the same way the four years that I was only nominally pastor and not at the church at all, under the different men who came and whom the people prayed into power. It went on the same way under Dr. Dixon's pastorate. It was not so much the men who were preaching as the people behind them who were praying that accomplished such great things for God. Then when I started around the world those people still followed me with their prayers; and it was reported when I came back, by one who claimed to know, that there were more than 102,000 persons who made a definite profession of accepting Christ in the different places I visited in those months that I was away. When I came back after my first eighteen months' absence, Dr. Dixon met me one day, and he said to me (this was before he became pastor of the church), "Torrey, when we heard the things that were done in Australia and elsewhere we were all surprised. We didn't think it was in you." He was perfectly right about that, it wasn't *in me*. Then he added, "But when I went out and supplied your church for a month and heard your people pray for you, I understood." Oh, any church can have a minister who is a man of power, a minister who is baptized and filled with the Holy Ghost, if they are willing to pay the price, and the price is prayer, much prayer, and much real prayer, prayer in the Holy Ghost.

3

WHAT PRAYER CAN DO FOR CHURCHES, AND FOR THE NATION, AND FOR ALL NATIONS

"With all prayer and supplication praying at all seasons in the Spirit, and watching thereunto in all perseverance and supplication for all the saints."—EPH. 6:18.

What a tremendous emphasis Paul here puts upon the importance and power of prayer, and upon the imperative need of intense earnestness and never wearying persistence in prayer. Listen to the text again: "With *all prayer* and *supplication* praying *at all seasons* in the Spirit, and *watching thereunto in all perseverance and supplication for all* the saints."

We have already seen in our studies some of the things of the first importance that are wrought by prayer, things that cannot be brought to pass in any other way. We have seen that true prayer will promote our own personal piety, and our individual holiness, our individual growth into the likeness of our Lord and Savior Jesus Christ, as almost nothing else, as nothing else but the study of the Word of God. We have seen that prayer will bring power into our work, that it is the privilege of every child of God to have the power of God manifested in his work in whatever line of service he is called, and that this power is obtained by prayer and in no other way. We have seen that prayer avails mightily for others as well as for ourselves; that we can accomplish more for the salvation of others by praying for them than we can in any other way, that prayer avails for the salvation of men and women who are so sunken in sin, and so far from God, that there seems no possible hope of their redemption. We have seen, furthermore, that prayer brings power to the minister of the Gospel, that any church can have a man of power for its pastor if they are willing to pay the price, and that the price is not a big salary but big praying.

We shall make other discoveries in this chapter—things that are greatly to be desired, that can be brought to pass by prayer and that can be brought to pass in no other way.

Andrew Murray has said, "God's child can conquer everything by prayer. Is it any wonder that Satan does his utmost to snatch that weapon from the Christian or to hinder him in the use of it?" Well, if the devil is doing "his utmost to snatch that weapon from the Christian or to hinder him in the use of it," I wish to do my utmost to restore that mighty weapon to the hands of the church, and to stir you up to use this weapon in mighty and victorious onslaught on Satan and his forces.

It is true that we have a terrific fight on our hands, that "our wrestling is not against flesh and blood, but against the principalities, against the powers, against the world-rulers of this darkness, against the spiritual hosts of wickedness in the heavenly places" (Eph. 6:12), but we can win this fight by prayer; for prayer brings God on the field and the devil is no match for Him. I say *we can win this fight, as terrible as it is and as mighty and cunning as our enemies are, by praying, and we cannot win it in any other way.* Men are constantly appearing who have discovered some new way of defeating the devil by some cunning scheme that they have devised, by the social gospel, for example, or by some other humanly devised method. But there is no new way that will win; the old way, the Bible way, the way of definite, determined and persistent prayer in the Holy Spirit, will win every time.

I. *Prayer Will Bring Blessing to Churches*

Let us now look at something else in addition to the important things already mentioned that prayer will do. Turn to I Thessalonians 3:11-13: "Now may our God and Father himself, and our Lord Jesus, direct our way unto you: and *the Lord make you to increase and abound in love* one toward another, and toward all men, even as we also do toward you: *to the end he may establish your hearts unblamable in holiness before our God and Father* at the coming of our Lord Jesus with all his saints."

In the last chapter we saw the church praying for Paul: in this passage we see Paul praying for the church. Prayer will bring blessing, definite and rich and immeasurable blessing, to the church; praying will do more to make the Church what it ought to be than anything else we can do. Prayer will do more to root out heresy than all the heresy trials ever held. Prayer will do more to straighten out tangles and misunderstandings and unhappy complications in the life of a church than all the councils and conferences ever held. Prayer will do more to bring a deep and lasting and sweeping revival, a revival that is real and lasting and altogether of the right sort, than all the organizations ever devised by man.

The history of the church of Jesus Christ on earth has been largely a history of revivals. When you read many of the church histories that have been written the impression that you naturally get is that the history of the church of Jesus Christ here on earth has been largely a history of misunderstandings, disputes, doctrinal differences and bitter conflicts; but, if you will study the history of the living church, you will find it has been largely a history of revivals. Humanly speaking, the church of Jesus Christ owes its very existence today to revivals. Time and time again the church has seemed to be on the verge of utter shipwreck; but just then God has sent a great revival and saved it. And if you will study the history of revivals you will find that every real revival in the church has been the result of prayer. There have been revivals without much preaching; there have been revivals with absolutely no organization; but there has never been a mighty revival without mighty praying.

Take the great revival that so marvelously blessed our nation in 1857. How did that revival come about? A humble city missionary in the city of New York, a man named Landfear, became greatly burdened because of the state of the church. He and two other men who were like-minded began to pray for a revival. Then they opened a daily noon-meeting for prayer and invited others. These meetings were poorly attended at first. On one occasion, if I remember correctly, there were only two persons present, and I think that on one occasion there was only one person present, this humble city missionary himself, this very obscure man Landfear, whose sisters I afterwards knew well and whose cousin was a member of the first church of which I was pastor. But soon the interest began to deepen and large crowds began to flock to the meetings for prayer. Such throngs came that it became necessary to appoint other prayer-meetings, and I have been told (and I think correctly told), that after a while prayer-meetings were held every hour of the day and night in New York City, and not only the churches were used for prayer-meetings but theatres and other public places. And these places were crowded with praying men and praying women. The fire spread from New York to Philadelphia and to other cities, and then swept over the entire country. A young man came into one of the meetings in Chicago on one occasion and said that he had just come back from a trip to the far west, and that at every place where he had stopped on the way back to Chicago prayer-meetings were being held.

In New York City, at one of the Presbyterian ministers' meetings, Dr. Gardiner Spring, who was perhaps at that time the most prominent minister in New York, said to the assembled brethren, "It is evident that a revival has come to us and we ministers must preach." Someone replied, "Well, if anyone must preach you must preach the first sermon, for you are the best qualified to do it of any man in the city." So it was announced that on a certain day Dr. Gardiner Spring would preach, but no more people came out to hear the preaching than came out to the prayer-meetings, so they stopped the preaching and went on praying. *The whole emphasis was on prayer,* and our whole nation was shaken by the power of God as it had never been shaken before, and perhaps has never been shaken since. That is the kind of a revival I am longing to see

44

here in our city; yes, throughout our whole land; yes, throughout the world. Not a revival where there is great preaching and marvelous singing and all kinds of bewildering antics by preachers or singers, or skillful managers or manipulators; but a revival where there is mighty praying and wonderful displays of the convicting and converting and regenerating power of the Holy Spirit in answer to prayer.

Don't come to me and tell me what this man or that man, or this woman or that woman, is doing that you think is wrong or that you think is right. Go to God and tell Him if you like; but it is far more important that you *pray* to Him. Pray, pray, pray for Him to bless your church and to bless other churches of your city, and to bless the whole land; yes, and to bless every land.

The news of what God was doing in 1857 in America spread to the north of Ireland, and the General Assembly of the Presbyterian Church of Ireland sent a Commission to America to study the work and to come back with a report. When they came back they gave to the next General Assembly a glowing report of what was being done in America. People began to pray that Ireland might also have a similar visitation from God.

Four men in the little town of Kells, in the North of Ireland, banded themselves together and met every Saturday night for prayer for a revival. They spent the whole night in prayer. They were humble men: one of them was a farmer, one was a blacksmith, one was a school teacher, and I do not recall what the fourth was, but I know he was in some humble sphere of life. When Mr. Alexander and I were holding meetings in London, and God was working there in great power, one of these four men, at that time living in Glasgow, sent his grandson down to London to consult with Mr. Alexander and myself and to observe the work and bring back a report to him as to whether it was a real work of God or not.

After these men had been praying for some time they went out to try and preach, but their attempt was a failure, so they went back and kept on praying. God heard their prayer and the fire of God fell, and the work went on in such marvelous power in some parts of Ireland that courts adjourned because there were no cases to try, jails were closed because there were no prisoners to incarcerate, and in some places even the grain stood ungarnered in the fields because men were so taken up with things of God and of eternity that they had no time to attend even to the things that ordinarily are so necessary. Many of the most notorious and hardened and hopeless sinners in the land were converted and thoroughly transformed.

Let me tell you how the revival came to Coleraine. I know something about that, because when Mr. Alexander and I were in Belfast, Ireland, in 1903, they were about to celebrate at Coleraine the forty-third anniversary of how the revival came to Coleraine, and they sent a committee down to Belfast to invite Mr. Alexander and myself to go up and celebrate the anniversary of the coming of the revival to Coleraine forty-three years before. We were unable to go; but I read very carefully the account of the revival as it was given by Rev. William Gibson, Moderator of the General Assembly of the Presbyterian Church in Ireland for 1860, in his book, *The Year of Grace.* It was reported on a certain day in Coleraine that three young men were coming to Coleraine that evening to hold an open air meeting in the market-place. At the appointed hour the ministers of the city went down to the market-place out of curiosity, to see what was done. To their amazement they saw the people pouring into the market-place from every quarter until there were no less than 15,000 people gathered together in the market-place. The ministers looked at one another in bewilderment and dismay and said, "We must preach, these young men can never deal with a vast throng like this."

So they put up four pulpits at the four corners of the market-place and a preacher ascended each pulpit. They had not been preaching long when a very solemn awe fell upon the entire throng, and soon in one section of the market-place there was a loud cry and a man fell to the ground under such overwhelming conviction of sin that he could not stand on his feet. He was carried out to the Town Hall that was not yet completed. Soon a cry arose in another part of the market-place and another man fell under the power of conviction of sin, and he too was taken to the Town Hall; then another, and then another, and then another fell in different parts of the market-place until conviction became so general that the meeting broke up and the ministers adjourned to the Town Hall to deal individually with stricken souls. The Presbyterian minister who tells the incident says that he was in the Town Hall all night dealing with souls overwhelmed with deep conviction of sin. When the morning dawned, this minister tells us, he started for his home, but as he went up the street he found people standing on their doorsteps waiting for him to pass, because there were people under conviction of sin in their homes and they wanted to invite him in to deal with them. He went into one home after another, and there were so many to deal with that the sun had set before he reached his own home. The whole town of Coleraine was so transformed and so impressed that in completing the Town Hall they put in an inscribed tablet dedicating the hall to the memory of the revival, and for every year of the forty-three years up to that time they were commemorating the coming of the revival to Coleraine; and I think they have kept up the commemoration annually to this present day.

I think it was at the close of the week of prayer in January, 1901, that Miss Strong, Superintendent of Women of the Bible Institute of Chicago, came to me and said, "Why not keep up these prayer-meetings at least once a week after the week of prayer is over, and pray for a world-wide revival?" This suggestion approved itself to the Faculty and we appointed a prayer-meeting every Saturday night from nine to ten o'clock (after the popular Bible class was over) at which people could gather to pray for just one thing—*a world-wide revival*. Three or four hundred gathered every Saturday night for that purpose, and God gave to us great liberty and great expectation in prayer. Soon we began to hear of the working of God in Japan and other lands, and yet the work was not as general as we wanted to see. People would come to me and to my colleague who was most intimately associated with me in the conduct of the meetings, and ask, "Has the revival come?"

We replied, "No, not as far as we know."

"When is it coming?"

"We do not know."

"How long are you going to keep praying?"

"Until it comes."

After we had been praying for some months two men from far away Australia appeared in our lecture room. After they had been attending the lectures for sometime they asked for a private conversation with me. They told me that in leaving Australia they had been commissioned to go to England, to Keswick and other places, and to other gatherings in America, and select someone to invite to Australia to conduct an evangelistic campaign. They said further that they had both agreed upon me: would I go? I replied, "I do not see how I can leave Chicago. I have the Bible Institute to look after, and also the Chicago Avenue Church (the Moody Church), and I do not see how I can possibly get away from Chicago."

"Well," they said, "you are coming to Australia." Some months passed by and I was in a Bible Conference in St. Louis and I received a letter from Australia asking me to cable my acceptance of their invitation, and that they would at once cable me the money to come. I laid the matter before the Conference and asked them to pray over it, and withdrew from the Conference to be alone in prayer. And God made it clear that I should go, and I so cabled them. When Mr. Alexander and I reached Australia we found that there was a group of about ten or twelve men who had been praying for years for a great revival in Australia. They had banded together to pray for "the big revival," as they called it in their prayers, to pray for the revival no matter how long it took. The group was led by the Rev. John McNeil, the author of *The Spirit-Filled Life,* but he had died before we reached Australia. A second member of the group, Rev. Allan Webb, died the first week of our meetings in Melbourne. He had come to Melbourne to assist in the meetings, and died on his knees in prayer. A third member of the group, even before we had been invited to Australia, had been given a vision of great crowds flocking to the Exposition Hall, people hanging on to the loaded street cars wherever they could; and when that vision was fulfilled

48

he came a long distance to Melbourne just to see with his own eyes what God had revealed to him before.

We also found that a lady in Melbourne had read a book on Prayer and had been very deeply impressed by one short sentence in the book, "pray through," and that she had organized prayer-meetings all over the city before we reached the place; indeed, we found when we reached Melbourne that there were 1,700 neighborhood prayer-meetings being held every week in Melbourne. We remained in that city four weeks. The first two weeks the meetings were held by many different pastors and evangelists in some forty or fifty different centers throughout the city, though meetings for the whole city were held at one o'clock, and two o'clock, and three o'clock each day in the Town Hall. The last two weeks, the meetings were all concentrated in the Exposition Hall, seating about 8,000 people. At the very first meeting in the Exposition Hall the crowd was so great that they swept the police before them, packed the building far beyond its proper capacity, and great crowds still could not get in. In the four weeks, 8,642 persons made a definite profession of having accepted the Lord Jesus Christ as their Savior. And when we went back to Melbourne some months later and held a meeting of the converts, 6,000 of them were present at that meeting, most of whom had already joined the church; and almost all those who had not united with the church as yet, promised to do so at once. The report of what God had done in Melbourne spread not only all over Australia, but to India, and England and Scotland and Ireland, and resulted in a wonderful work of God in the leading cities of England, Scotland and Ireland, and the whole world-wide work was the outcome of the prayer-meetings held in Chicago, and of the prayers of the little group of men in Australia.

The great Welsh revival in 1904, the beginning of which I was an eye-witness, came in a similar way. Mr. Alexander and I had been invited to Cardiff, Wales, for a month's mission. The announcement that we were going there was made about a year before we went, and prayer began to go up all over England and Scotland and Wales that God would send a revival not only to Cardiff but to all Wales. When we reached Cardiff we found that for almost a year they had been holding a prayer-meeting from six to seven every morning in Penarth, a suburb of Cardiff, praying for a great revival. For the first two weeks or so things dragged. Great crowds came and there was great enthusiasm in the singing, but we could not get the people to do personal work. Then we appointed *a day of fasting and prayer,* and the day was observed in other parts of Wales as well as in Cardiff.

In one place Seth Joshua, who was afterwards so greatly used in the revival, was the leading figure and had charge of the meeting, and wrote me a most glowing and cheerful account of what God had done in that place on that day. I think it was on that very day that he was kneeling beside Evan Roberts, and as he prayed the power of God fell upon Evan Roberts. The power of God came down in Cardiff in such a wonderful way that when Mr. Alexander and I were compelled to leave at the end of the month to keep an engagement in Liverpool, the meetings went right on without us and they went on for one whole year—meetings every night for a whole year, and multitudes were converted. From Cardiff the fire spread up and down the valleys of Wales. Soon after we had reached Liverpool, the next city that we visited, I received a letter from the minister who was Secretary of our mission in Cardiff, in which he said that his assistant had gone out the preceding Sunday night up one of the valleys of Wales and that as he preached the power of God fell on him and 100 persons were converted while he was preaching. The fire spread over the entire country under Evan Roberts and others, and it is said that more than 100,000 souls were converted in twelve months.

That is what we need more than anything else today, in our own land and in all lands—a mighty outpouring of the Spirit of God. The most fundamental trouble with most of our present-day so-called revivals is that *they are man-made and not God-sent.* They are worked up (I almost said faked up) by man's cunningly devised machinery—not prayed down. Oh, for an old-time revival, a revival that is really and not spuriously of the Pentecostal pattern—for that revival was born of a

50

fourteen days prayer-meeting. But let us not merely sigh for it; let us cry for it, cry to God, cry long and cry loud if need be, and then it will surely come.

II. *Prayer Will Bring Blessing and Victory to Foreign Missions*

"But when he saw the multitudes, he was moved with compassion for them, because they were distressed and scattered, as sheep not having a shepherd. Then said he unto his disciples, The harvest indeed is plenteous, but the labourers are few. *Pray ye therefore* the Lord of the harvest, that he send forth labourers into his harvest" (Matt. 9:36-38 R. V.). Here we see from our Lord's own teaching that prayer will bring blessing to foreign missions. It will get the needed men and women, and the right kind of men and women, for the work in all the fields which are now white for the harvest in many lands. It will also bring blessing and power to the men and women who go to the field. *The greatest need of foreign missions today is prayer.* It is true that men are greatly needed, and it is true that money is needed; but prayer is needed far more. When we pray as we ought the men and the women will come, and the money will come. Even though men came in crowds, without prayer they would be of no use; they will be of no use whatever unless they are backed by prayer.

In this country men of great force of character and mind have greatly stirred students to an interest in foreign missions, and have gathered large numbers of men and women for the foreign field, without much prayer; and these men and women, though gifted, some of them greatly talented, have oftentimes been an actual curse to the work. It is my conviction, founded upon quite a little observation, that the work of foreign missions would be far better off today if these men had gone into secular work and left missions alone. The results of their work have been most sinister. I have seen much of it with my own eyes in China and elsewhere, and I am convinced that one of the most discouraging problems that faces foreign mission work has arisen from the large number of men and women who have gone into the foreign work not because they were sent of God in answer to prayer, but because they were stirred up by a man of attractive personality and rare power.

What we have said of men is just as true of money. No matter how much money may be put into foreign missions, the money will be of no real use unless the men and women whom the money sends out are backed by prayer. Indeed, without prayer, the money will be a curse rather than a blessing. Probably no other missionary society in all this world's history ever accomplished as much good, all things considered (that is of real and lasting value), as the China Inland Mission; and that is so because this Mission was born of so much prayer and backed by so much prayer.

But what shall we pray for in connection with foreign missions?

1. First of all *we should pray,* just as the words of our Lord Jesus we are studying command us to pray, *for men and women.* Listen to our Lord's words again, "The harvest indeed is plenteous, but the labourers are few. Pray ye therefore the Lord of the harvest, that *he* send forth labourers into *his* harvest." It is not so much a large number of men and women who are needed, it is the right kind of men and women. A large number of men and women are needed, no question about that. The fields were never so white for the harvest before as they are today, and the laborers are indeed few; but the greatest need is *the right kind of men and women. Missions in China and elsewhere would be far better off today if many of the men and women who have gone out had remained at home.* Earnest-minded men and women from this country who visited China and were brought in close contact with some of the young men and women that were being poured into China by certain missionary societies were appalled at the thought that men and women of this type should be sent out for foreign mission work. Many of the older missionaries who have made great sacrifices for the work, and by much effort and prayer have gathered together bodies of believers who really know the Lord, trembled as they thought what the influence of this type of missionaries would be upon the doctrine and the life of the Chinese converts. Many of the Christian Chinese

52

themselves felt they must protest against the teaching and the manner of life of these would-be missionaries.

2. In the second place, *We should pray for the missionaries who have already gone out.* We have already seen how much prayer does to make a minister of the Gospel what he ought to be. If possible, prayer is even more effective in making missionaries what they ought to be, and the neglect of prayer on the part of the people at home has much to do with the comparative failure of many of the missionaries on the field. Every Christian at home should have some definite missionaries in the field for whom he is praying definitely, constantly, persistently, and intensely. The man or woman at home who prays, often has as much to do with the effectiveness of the missionary on the field, and consequently with the results of his labors, as the missionary himself.

3. In the third place, *We should pray for the outpouring of the Spirit on different fields.* Oh, how much genuine revivals of religion in the power of the Holy Spirit are needed in the various missionary fields of the world. And revivals on the foreign field come in exactly the same way we have just seen revivals come at home— in answer to prayer. That could be proved by many illustrations. Mr. Finney tells of a mighty man of prayer who was interested not only in the work at home, but abroad; and after his death his diary was found and in examining it it was found that on certain days it was recorded that he had a great burden of prayer for some specific foreign missionary field, and upon inquiry it was found that in each instance revivals on the foreign field had followed this man's insistent intercession, and followed in the exact order of his petitions as recorded in his diary. Many of us are tempted to criticize the foreign work because of the meagerness of the results, but ought not our criticism to begin with ourselves? May it not be that the meagerness of the results is the consequence of the meagerness of our own prayer? At all events we can increase the blessed and glorious results of the work in foreign fields by giving more time to real prayer here at home.

4. In the fourth place, *We should pray for the native converts.* It is difficult for us to realize how many and

how great are the obstacles put in the way of a native convert's standing steadfast in the new life, and the difficulties that lie in the way of his living such a life as a Christian ought to live, in the atmosphere that he daily breathes. Many of the converts in many fields are men and women of an unusually high character. My son has told me that some of the Christian Chinese he knows intimately put him to shame by their clearness of understanding of the deep things of God and by the Christlikeness and devotion of their lives. But while this is true, we should never forget that it is far more difficult for one converted in a heathen land to lead the life a Christian ought to live than it is for one converted in this land, and, therefore, the converts greatly need our prayers. And our prayer "availeth much in its working" in the lives of those who are won to Christ in the foreign field.

5. In the fifth place, *We should pray for the native churches.* We should not only pray for the converts as individuals, but for the churches as organizations. Every church has its peculiar problems. Take for example the Church of Christ in Korea. It is difficult for anyone who has not visited that land, so wonderfully favored of God in missionary work and at the same time so amazingly resisted by the devil in various ways, to realize how much the Church of Christ in Korea needs the prayers of those in the home land who believe in Christ and in prayer. And so also do the churches in Africa and India, and elsewhere, greatly need our prayers here at home.

6. In the sixth place, *We should pray for the secretaries and official members of the various boards here at home.*

7. In the seventh place and finally, *We should pray for money.* Many of the boards and missionary societies are in extreme distress for funds today. This is true even of boards and councils of whose loyalty to the faith there is no question: they are in great need of increased gifts. The way to get the money is to pray for it: and not only for those who are immediately responsible for the money to pray for it, but for us all to pray for it. Very likely, if we pray as we ought, God will give us to see that we ourselves ought to go down into

54

our own pockets as we never have done to aid in answering our own prayers.

There are many other definite things, and things greatly to be desired, that definite and determined prayer will bring to pass; but I wish to concentrate your attention on just these two things in this chapter: First, that prayer will bring blessing to the churches; and second, that prayer will bring blessing and victory to foreign missions.

Oh, how much we need the blessing that includes all other blessings for the church, a great, deep, thoroughgoing, widespread revival. And how we need larger blessing and more thoroughgoing victory in the work of foreign missions. We can have both if we will pay the price; and the price is prayer—real prayer, determined prayer, protracted prayer, heart-wringing, crying to God in the power of the Holy Spirit

4

HOW TO PRAY SO AS TO GET
WHAT YOU ASK

*"But prayer was made earnestly of the church unto
God for him."*—ACTS 12:5 R. V.

Our subject is, "How to pray so as to get what
you ask." I can think of nothing more important than
that to discuss with you. Suppose it had been announced that I was to tell the business men of Los
Angeles how they could go to any bank in the city and
get all the financial accommodation they desired any
day in the year, and suppose, also, that I really knew
that secret and could really tell it. Do you think that the
business men of that city would consider it important? It would be difficult to think of anything they
would consider more important! But praying is going to
the bank, going to the bank that has the largest capital
of any bank in the universe, the Bank of Heaven, a
bank whose capital is absolutely unlimited. And if I
can show you how you can go to the Bank of Heaven
any day in the year, and any hour of the day or night,
and get from that bank all that you desire, that will
certainly be of incalculable importance.

Now the Bible tells us that very thing. It tells us how
we can go to the Bank of Heaven, how we can go to
God in prayer any day of the year and any hour of the
day or night, and get from God the very things that we
ask. What the Bible teaches along this line has been put
to the test of practical experiment by tens of thousands
of people, and has been found in their own experience

to be absolutely true. And that is what we are about to discover in God's own Word.

In Acts 12 we have the record of a most remarkable prayer, remarkable because of what was asked for and remarkable because of the results of the asking. King Herod had killed James, the brother of John. This greatly "pleased the Jews"; so he proceeded further to arrest the leader of the whole apostolic company, the Apostle Peter, with the intention of killing him also. But the arrest was made during Passover Week, the Holy Week of the Jews; and, while the Jews were perfectly willing to have Peter assassinated, even eager, they were not willing to have their Holy Week desecrated by his violent death. So Peter was cast into prison to be kept until the Passover Week was over, and then to be executed. The Passover Week was nearly over; it was the last night of the Passover Week. Early the next morning Peter was to be taken out and beheaded.

There seemed to be little hope for Peter, indeed no hope at all. He was in a secure dungeon, in an impregnable fortress, guarded by sixteen soldiers, and chained by each wrist to a soldier who slept on either side of him. There appeared to be no hope whatever for Peter. But the Christians in Jerusalem undertook to get Peter out of his perilous position, to completely deliver him. How did they go about it? Did they organize a mob and storm the castle? No, there was no hope whatever of success along that line; the castle was impregnable against any mob, and, furthermore it was garrisoned by trained Roman soldiers who would be more than a match for any mob. Did they circulate a petition and get the names of the leading Christians in Jerusalem signed to it to present to Herod, asking that he would release Peter? No. That might have had weight, for the Christians in Jerusalem at that time were numbered by the thousands and among them were not a few influential persons. A petition signed by so many people and by people of such weight, would have had influence with a wily politician such as Herod. But they did not attempt that method of deliverance. Did they take up a collection and gather a large amount of money from the believers in Jerusalem to bribe Herod to release Peter? Quite likely that might have proved successful, for

Herod was open to that method of approach. But they did not do that.

What did they do? They *held a prayer-meeting* to pray Peter out of prison. Was anything apparently more futile and ridiculous ever undertaken by a company of fanatics? Praying a man so securely incarcerated, and so near his execution, out of prison? If the enemies of Peter and the church had known of that attempt they doubtless would have been greatly amused, and laughed at the thought of these fanatical Christians praying Peter out of prison. Doubtless they would have said to one another, "We'll see what will become of the prayers of these fool Christians."

But the attempt to pray Peter out of prison was entirely successful. Apparently Peter himself had no fears, but he was calmly resting in God; for he was fast asleep on the very eve of his proposed execution. While Peter was sound asleep, guarded by the sixteen soldiers, chained to a soldier sleeping on either side of him, suddenly there shone in the prison a light, a light from Heaven; and there could have been seen standing by Peter "an angel of God." The angel "smote Peter on the side" as he slept and awakened him and said, "Arise up quickly." Instantly Peter's chains fell from his hands and he arose to his feet. The angel said to him, "Gird thyself, and bind on thy sandals." Peter did so, and then the angel said, "Cast thy garment about thee, and follow me." Peter, dazed and wondering, thought he was dreaming; but he was wise enough to obey God even in his sleep and he went out and followed the angel, though he "thought he saw a vision." The soldiers were all asleep, but unprevented Peter passed the first guard and the second guard and came to the strong iron gate that led into the city. Moved by the finger of God, the gate "opened to them of its own accord." They went out and silently passed through one street.

Now Peter was safe and the angel left him. Standing there in the cold night air, Peter came to himself. He realized that he was not dreaming, and said, "Now I know of a truth, that the Lord has sent forth his angel to deliver me out of the hand of Herod, and from all the expectation of the people of the Jews." Stopping a few moments to reflect, he said to himself, "There is a

58

prayer-meeting going on. It must be at Mark's mother's house; I will go there."

Soon the pray-ers were startled by a heavy pounding at the outside gate of Mark's mother's home. There was a little servant girl named Rhoda kneeling among the pray-ers. Instantly she sprang to her feet and rushed to the gate, saying to herself, "That's Peter! That's Peter! I knew God would hear our prayers. God has delivered him, and he is at the gate." Reaching the gate she excitedly cried, "Is that you, Peter?" "Yes." Too excited even to open the gate, she left Peter standing outside. She dashed back and said to the startled prayers, "Our prayers are answered—Peter is at the gate."

"Oh, Rhoda, you are crazy," cried the unbelieving company.

"No," Rhoda said, "I am not crazy. It is Peter. God has answered our prayers. I know his voice. I knew he would come and he is here."

Then they all cried, "It is not Peter, it is his ghost. He has been killed in the night and his ghost has come around and is rapping at the gate." But Peter kept on knocking and they opened the gate, and there stood Peter, the living evidence that God had answered their prayer.

By the way, have you ever noticed that among all the company that were present at that prayer-meeting only one person is mentioned by name, and that one person only a servant girl, Rhoda? Doubtless the bishops and elders of the church in Jerusalem were there, but not a single name of theirs has gone down. Probably some of the leading people of Jerusalem, who had now become Christians, were there, but not a single name is mentioned. "Rhoda," and Rhoda only. Why? Because Rhoda was the only one who really had faith and was therefore the only one worth mentioning, even though she was only a servant girl. "Rhoda" means rose, and this Rhoda was a rose who was very fragrant to God, although she was only a servant girl; for there is no sweeter fragrance to God than the fragrance of faith.

Now if we can find out how these people prayed, then we shall know just how we too can pray so as to get what we ask. In the fifth verse we are told exactly how they prayed. Let me read it to you. "Prayer was made *without ceasing of the church unto God for him.*" The whole secret of prevailing prayer, the prayer that gets what it asks, is found in four phrases in this brief description of their prayer. The first phrase is, "Without ceasing." The second, "Of the church." The third, "Unto God." The fourth, "For him."

I. *"Unto God"*

Let us take up these four phrases and study them. We take up first the third phrase, for it is really the most important one, *"Unto God."* The prayer that gets what it asks is the prayer that is *unto God*. But someone will say, "Is not all prayer unto God?" No. Comparatively few of the prayers that go up from this earth today are really unto God. I sometimes think that not one prayer in a hundred is really "unto God." You ask, "What do you mean?" I mean exactly what I say, that not one prayer in a hundred is really unto God. "Oh," you say, "I know what you mean. You are talking about the prayers of the heathen unto their idols and their false gods." No, I mean the prayers of people who call themselves Christians. I do not think that one in a hundred of them are really unto God. "Oh," you say, "I know what you mean. You are talking of the prayers of the Roman Catholics unto the Virgin Mary and unto the saints." No, I mean the prayers of people who call themselves Protestants. I do not believe that one in a hundred of the prayers of Protestant believers are really *unto God*. "What do you mean?" you ask. I mean exactly what I say.

Stop a moment and think. Is it not often the case when men stand up to pray in public, or kneel down to pray in private, that they are thinking far more of what they are asking for than they are of the great God who made heaven and earth, and who has all power, of whom they are asking it? Is it not often the case that in our prayers we are not thinking much either of what we are asking for or of Him from whom we are asking it, but our thoughts are wandering off wool gathering everywhere? We take the name of God upon our lips but there is no real conscious approach to God in our hearts. We are really taking the name of God in vain

60

while we fancy we are praying to Him. If there is to be any power in our prayer, if our prayer is to get anything, the first thing to be sure of when we pray is that we have really come into the presence of God, and are really speaking to Him. We should never utter one syllable of prayer, either in public or in private, until we are definitely conscious that we have come into the presence of God and are actually praying to Him. Oh, let those two words, "Unto God," *"Unto God,"* "UNTO GOD," sink deep into your heart; and from this time on never pray, never utter one syllable of prayer, until you are sure that you have come into the presence of God and are really talking to Him.

There was a time when I had wandered far from God, and had definitely decided that I would not accept Jesus Christ; nevertheless, I prayed every night. I had come to a place where I doubted whether the Bible was the Word of God, and whether Jesus Christ was the Son of God, and even doubted whether there were a personal God; nevertheless, I prayed every night. I am glad that I was brought up that way, and that the habit of prayer was so instilled into me that it became habitual; for it was along that line that I came back out of the darkness of agnosticism into the clear light of an intelligent faith in God and His Word. Nevertheless, prayer was largely a mere matter of form. There was little real thought of God, and no real approach to God. And even after I was converted, yes, even after I had entered the ministry, prayer was largely a matter of form. But the day came when I realized what real prayer meant, realized that prayer was having an audience with God, actually coming into the presence of God and asking and getting things from Him. And the realization of that fact transformed my prayer life. Before that, prayer had been a mere duty, and sometimes a very irksome duty, but from that time on prayer has been not merely a duty but a privilege, one of the most highly esteemed privileges of life. Before that the thought I had was, "How much time must I spend in prayer?" The thought that now possesses me is, "How much time may I spend in prayer without neglecting the other privileges and duties of life?"

Suppose some Englishman were summoned to Buckingham Palace to meet the Queen. He answers the summons and is waiting in the anteroom to be ushered into her presence. What do you think that man would say to himself as he waited to be brought in? Do you think he would say, "I wonder how much time I must spend with the Queen?" No, indeed; he would rather think, "I wonder how much time the Queen will give me." But prayer is having an audience with the King of kings, that eternal, omnipotent King in comparison with whom all earthly kings and queens are as nothing; and would any intelligent person who realizes that fact ever ask himself, "How much time must I spend in prayer?" No, our thought will be, "How much time may I spend in prayer, how much time will the King give me?"

So let these two words, "Unto God," sink deep into your heart and govern your prayer life from this day on. Whenever you kneel in prayer, or stand in prayer, whether it be in public or in private, be absolutely sure before you utter a syllable that you have actually come into the presence of God and are really speaking to Him. Oh, it is a wondrous secret.

But at this point a question arises. How can we come into the presence of God, and how can we be sure that we have come into the presence of God, and that we are really talking to Him? Some years ago I was speaking upon this verse of Scripture in Chicago, and at the close of the address an intelligent Christian woman, one of the most intelligent and deeply spiritual women I ever knew, came to me and said, "Mr. Torrey, I like that thought of 'unto God,' but how can we come into the presence of God and how can we be absolutely sure that we have come into the presence of God, and that we are really talking to Him?" It was a wise question and a question of great importance; and it is clearly answered in the Word of God. There are two parts to the answer.

1. You will find the first part of the answer in Hebrews 10:19, "Having therefore, brethren, boldness to enter into the holiest *by the blood of Jesus*." That is the first part of the answer. We come into the presence of God "by the blood of Jesus": and we can come into the presence of God in no other way. Just what does that mean? It means this: You and I are sinners, the

best of us are great sinners, and God is infinitely holy, so holy that even the Seraphim, those wonderful *"burning ones"* (for that is what Seraphim means), burning in their own intense holiness, must veil their faces and their feet in His presence (Isaiah 6:2). But our sins have been laid upon another, upon the Lord Jesus when He died upon the cross of Calvary and made a perfect atonement for our sins. When He died there He took our place, the place of rejection by God, the place of the "curse," and the moment we accept Him and believe in God's testimony concerning His blood, that by His shed blood He made perfect atonement for our sin, and trust God to forgive and justify us because the Lord Jesus died in our place, that moment our sins are forgiven and we are reckoned righteous and enter into a place above the Seraphim, the place of God's only and perfect Son, Jesus Christ.

And we do not need to veil our faces or our feet when we come into His presence, for we are made perfectly "accepted in the Beloved" (Eph. 1:6). To "enter into the holiest" then, to come into the very presence of God, *"by the blood of Jesus,"* means that when we draw near to God we should give up any and every thought that we have any acceptability before God in ourselves, we must realize that we are miserable sinners, but we must also believe that every sin of ours has been atoned for *by the shed blood of Jesus Christ,* and therefore we come "with boldness" into the very presence of God, "into the holiest, by the blood of Jesus." The best man or woman on earth cannot come into the presence of God on the ground of any merit of his own, not for one moment; nor can he get anything from God on the ground of his own goodness, not even the smallest blessing. But *on the ground of the shed blood of Jesus Christ the vilest sinner who ever walked this earth, who has turned from his sin and accepted Jesus Christ and trusts in the shed blood as the ground of his acceptance before God, can come into the presence of God any day of the year, and any hour of the day or night, and with perfect boldness speak out every longing of his heart and get what he asks from God.* Isn't that wonderful? Yes, and, thank God, it is true.

The Christian Scientist cannot really pray. What he calls prayer is simply meditation or concentration of thought. It is not asking a personal God for a definite blessing; indeed, Mrs. Eddy denied the existence of a personal God and she denied the atoning efficacy of the blood. She said that the blood of Jesus Christ when it was shed on the cross of Calvary, did no more good than when it was running in His veins. So a Christian Scientist cannot really pray; he is not on praying ground.

Neither can a Unitarian really pray. Oh, he can take the name of God upon his lips and call Him Father, and say beautiful words, but there is no real approach to God. Our Lord Jesus Christ Himself said, "I am the Way, the Truth, and the Life: no man cometh unto the Father, but by (more literally, through) Me." Some years ago I was on a committee in Chicago of three persons, one of whom was a leading Unitarian minister of the city. He was a charming man in many ways. One day at the close of our committee meeting this Unitarian minister turned to me and said, "Brother Torrey, I often come to your church to hear you."

I replied, "I am very glad to hear it."

Then he continued, "I specially love to go to your prayer-meetings. Often of a Friday night I drop into your prayer-meeting and sit down by the door, and I greatly enjoy it."

I replied, "I am glad that you do. But tell me something. Why don't you have a prayer-meeting in your own church?"

"Well," he said, "you have asked me an honest question and I will give you an honest answer. Because I can't. I have tried it and it has failed every time." Of course it failed, they had no ground of approach to God—they denied the atoning blood.

But there is many a supposedly orthodox Christian, and often in these days even supposedly orthodox ministers, who deny the atoning blood. They do not believe that the forgiveness of our sins is solely and entirely on the ground of the shedding of Jesus' blood as an atonement for sin on our behalf on the cross of Calvary; *therefore, they cannot really pray.* There are some who call the theology that insists upon the truth so very

64

clearly taught in the Word of God (of the substitution-
ary character of Christ's death and that we are saved by
the shedding of His blood) a "theology of the sham-
bles" (that is, of the butcher shop).

Mr. Alexander and I were holding meetings in the
Royal Albert Hall in London. I received through the
mail one day one of our hymn books that some man
had taken from the meeting. He had gone through it
and cut out every reference to the blood of Christ. With
the hymn book was an accompanying letter, and in this
letter the man said, "I have gone through your hymn
book and cut out every reference to the blood in every
place where it is found, and I am sending this hymn
book back to you. Now sing your hymns this way with
the blood left out and there will be some sense in
them." I took the hymn book to the meeting with me
that afternoon and displayed it; it was a sadly mutilated
book. I read the man's letter, and then I said, "No, I
will not cut the blood out of my hymnology, and I will
not cut the blood out of my theology, for when I cut
the blood out of my hymnology and my theology I will
have to cut all access to God out of my experience."
No, you cannot approach God on any other ground
than the shed blood, and until you believe in the blood
of Jesus Christ as a perfect atonement for your sins,
and as the only ground upon which you can find forgiveness and justification, real prayer is an impossibil-
ity.

2. You will find the second part of the answer to the
question, "How can we come into the presence of God
and how can we be sure that we have come into His
presence?" in Ephesians 2:18, "For through him we
both have our access *in one Spirit* unto the Father."
Here we have the same thought repeated, that it is
"through Him." That is, through Jesus Christ, we have
our access to the Father; but we have an additional
thought also, the thought that while we come into the
presence of God *through* Jesus Christ, we come "in"
the One Spirit, that is the Holy Spirit. Just what does
that mean? It means this: It is the work of the Holy
Spirit, when you and I pray, to take us by the hand as
it were and lead us into the very presence of God and
introduce us to Him, and to *make God real to us as* we

65

pray. The Greek word translated "access" is the exact equivalent in its etymology of the word "introduction," which is really a Latin word transliterated into English.

It is the work of the Holy Spirit to introduce us to God, that is, to lead us into God's presence, and to make God real to us as we pray (or return thanks, or worship). And when we pray, in order that we may really come into the presence of God and be sure that we have come into His presence, we must look to the Holy Spirit to make God real to us.

Have you never had this experience—that when you knelt to pray it seemed as if there were no one there, as if you were just talking into the air, or into empty space? What shall we do at such a time as that? Shall we stop praying and wait until some time when we feel like praying? No, when we least feel like praying, and when God is least real to us, that is the time we most need to pray. What shall we do then? Simply be quiet and look up to God and ask God to fulfill His promise and to send His Holy Spirit to lead us into His presence and to make Him real to us. Then wait and expect. And He will come. He will take us into God's presence, and He will make God real to us. I can testify today that some of the most wonderful seasons of prayer I have ever had, have been times when as I first knelt to pray I had no real sense of God. There seemed to be no one there, I seemed as if I were talking into empty space; and then I have just looked up to God and asked Him and trusted Him to send His Holy Spirit to teach me to pray, to lead me into His presence, and to make Him real to me, and the Spirit has come, and He has made God so real to me that it almost seemed that if I opened my eyes I could see Him, in fact I did see Him with the eyes of my soul.

One night at the close of a sermon in Chicago in one of the churches on the South Side, I went down the aisle to speak to different individuals. I stepped up to a middle-aged man and asked him, "Are you a Christian?"

"No," he replied, "I am an infidel. Did you ever see God?"

I quickly replied, "Yes, I have seen God."

The man was startled and silenced. Did I mean that

I had seen God with these eyes of my body? No. But, thank God, I have two pairs of eyes; not only does my body have eyes, but my spirit also has eyes. I pity the person who has only one pair of eyes, no matter how good those eyes are. I thank God I have two pairs of eyes, these bodily eyes with which I see you, and the eyes of my spirit with which I see God. God has given me wonderful eyes for my body, that at sixty-seven years of age I have never had to wear glasses. I do not know what it means to have my eyes weary or painful under any circumstances. But I will gladly give up my physical eyes rather than those other eyes that God has given me, the eyes with which I see God.

This then is the way to come into the presence of God and to be sure that we have come into His presence: First, to come by the blood; second, to come in the Holy Spirit, looking to the Holy Spirit to lead us into the presence of God, and to make God real to us.

Let me call your attention in passing to the great practical importance of the doctrine of the Trinity. There are many who think that the doctrine of the Trinity is a purely abstract, metaphysical and utterly impractical doctrine. Not at all. It involves our whole spiritual life, and it is of the highest importance in the practical matter of praying. We need God the Father to pray *to;* we need Jesus Christ the Son to pray *through;* and we need the Holy Spirit to pray *in.* It is the prayer that is to God the Father, through Jesus Christ the Son, under the guidance and in the power of the Holy Spirit, that God the Father answers.

II. *With Intense Earnestness*

Now let us consider another of the four phrases used in Acts 12:5, that contain the whole secret of prevailing prayer. The two words "without ceasing," "Prayer was made *without ceasing* of the church unto God for him." If you have the Revised Version you will notice that it reads differently, that it reads in this way, "Prayer was made *earnestly* of the church unto God for him." The word "earnestly" comes far nearer giving the force of the original than the words "without ceasing" but even earnestly does not give the full force of the

67

Greek word used. The Greek word is "ektenōs," and it means literally *"stretched-out-edly."* You see how King James' translators came to translate it "without ceasing." They thought of the prayer as stretched out a long time, unceasing prayer. But that is not the thought at all. The Greek word is never used in that sense anywhere in the New Testament. And I do not know of a place in Greek literature outside of the Bible where it is so used. The word is a pictorial word, as so many Bible words are. It represents the soul stretched out in the intensity of its earnestness toward God.

Did you ever see a foot race? The racers are all toeing the mark waiting for the starter to say "go," or to shoot the starting pistol as a signal to go. As the critical moment approaches everything about the runners becomes more and more tense, until when the word "go" comes, or the revolver cracks, they go charging down the track with every nerve and muscle stretched toward yonder goal, and sometimes the veins stand out on their foreheads like whipcords—every runner wants to be the winner. That is the picture, the soul stretched out in intense earnestness toward God.

It is the same word that is used in the comparative mood in Luke 22:44, where we read, "And being in an agony he prayed *more earnestly* (literally, more stretched-out-edly); and his sweat was as it were great drops of blood falling down to the ground." The thought is, as I have pointed out, of the soul being stretched out toward God in intense earnestness of desire.

Probably the most accurate translation that could be given in a single word would be "intensely." "Prayer was made *intensely* of the church unto God for him." In fact the word "intensely" is from the same root, only it has a different prefix. In the 1911 Bible the passage is translated *"Instant and earnest* prayer was made of the church unto God for him," which is not a bad paraphrase though it is not a translation. And "intensely earnest prayer was made of the church unto God for him," would be an even better rendering.

It is the *intensely* earnest prayer to which God pays attention, and which He answers. This thought comes out again and again in the Bible. We find it even in the

Old Testament, in Jeremiah 29:13, "Ye shall seek me, and find me, when ye shall *search* for me *with all your heart.*" We here discover the reason why so many of our prayers are unheard by God. There is so little heart in them, so little intensity of desire for the thing asked, that there is no reason why God should pay any attention to them. Did you pray this morning? Doubtless almost every one of you would reply, "Yes, I did." Then suppose I ask you again, "For what did you pray this morning?" I fear that some of you would hesitate and ponder and then have to say, "Really, I forget what I did pray for this morning." Well, then, God will forget to answer. But if I should ask some of you if you prayed this morning you would say, "Yes." Then if I asked you for what you prayed you could tell me at once, for you always pray for the same thing. You have just a little rote of prayer that you go through each morning or each night. You fall on your knees, go through your little prayer automatically, scarcely thinking of what you are saying, in fact oftentimes you do not think of what you are saying but are thinking of a dozen other things while you are repeating your prayer. Such prayer is profanity, taking the name of God in vain.

When Mrs. Torrey and I were in India, she went up to Darjeeling, in the Himalayas, on the borders of Tibet. I was unable to go because of being so busy with meetings in Calcutta. When she came back she brought with her a Tibetan praying wheel. It is a little round brass cup on the top of a stick, and the cup revolves when the stick is whirled. The Tibetan writes out his prayers, drops them into the cup, and then he whirls the stick and the wheel goes round and the prayers are said. That is just the way a great many Americans pray—only the wheel is in their head instead of being on the top of a stick. They kneel down and rattle through a rote of prayer, day after day the same thing, with scarcely any thought of what they are praying about. That kind of prayer is profanity, "taking the name of God in vain," and it has no power whatever with God. It is a pure waste of time, or worse than a waste of time.

But if I should ask some of you what you prayed for

this morning you could tell me, for as you were in prayer the Spirit of God came upon you and with a great heartache of intensity of desire you cried to God for that thing that you must have. Well, God will hear your prayer and give you what you asked.

If we are to pray with power we must pray with intense earnestness, throwing our whole soul into the prayer. This thought comes out again and again in the Bible. For example, we find it in Romans 15:30, "Now I beseech you, brethren, for the Lord Jesus Christ's sake, and for the love of the Spirit, that ye *strive together* with me in your prayers to God for me." The word translated "strive together" in this verse is "sunagonizo." "Agonizo" means to "contend" or "strive" or "wrestle" or "fight." And this verse could be properly translated, "Now I beseech you, brethren, for the Lord Jesus Christ's sake, and for the love of the Spirit, that ye wrestle together with me in your prayers to God for me."

We hear a great deal in these days about "the rest of faith," by which men usually mean that we should take things very calmly in our Christian life, and when we pray we should simply come into God's presence as a little child and quietly and trustfully ask Him for the thing desired and count it ours, and go away calmly and reckon the thing ours. Now there is a truth in that, a great truth; but it is only one side of the truth, and a truth usually has two sides. The other side of the truth is this, that there is not only "the rest of faith" but there is also the "fight of faith," and my Bible has more to say about "the fight of faith" than it does about "the rest of faith." The thought of wrestling or fighting in prayer is not the thought that we have to wrestle with God to make God willing to grant our prayers. No, "our wrestling is . . . against the principalities, against the powers, against the world rulers of this darkness, against the spiritual hosts of wickedness in the heavenly places" (Eph. 6:12), against the devil and all his mighty forces, and there is no place where the devil so resists us as when we pray. Sometimes when we pray it seems as if all the forces of hell sweep in between us and God. What shall we do? Give up? No! A thousand times, No! Fight the thing through on your knees, wrestle in your prayer to God, and win.

Some years ago I was attending a Bible conference in Dr. James H. Brooks' old church in St. Louis. On the program was one of the most distinguished and most gifted Bible teachers America ever produced, and he was speaking this day on "The Rest of Faith." In his address he said, "I challenge anyone to show me a single passage in the Bible where we are told to wrestle in prayer." Now one speaker does not like to contradict another, but here was a challenge and there I was sitting on the platform. I was obliged to take it up. So I said in a low voice, "Romans 15:30, brother." He was a good enough Greek scholar to know that I had him, and what is more rare, he was honest enough to own it up on the spot. Yes, the Bible bids us "wrestle in prayer" and it is the prayer in which we actually wrestle in the power of the Holy Spirit that wins out with God. The word which is the root of the word translated "strive together," is *agōnē*, from which our word agony comes. In fact, in Luke 22:44, to which I have already referred, this is the very word that is translated agony, "And being in an *agony* he prayed more earnestly: and his sweat was as it were great drops of blood falling to the ground." Oh, that we might have more agonizing prayer.

Turn now to Colossians 4:12, 13, and you will find the same thought again, put in other words, "Epaphras, who is one of you, a servant of Christ, saluteth you, always *labouring fervently for you* (The Revised Version translates instead of *'laboring fervently* for you,' *'striving* for you,' the same word as in Romans 15:30) in prayers, that ye may stand perfect and complete in all the will of God. For I bear him record, that he hath a *great zeal* for you." The words translated "great zeal" in this version are translated in the Revised Version, "much labor," which is an accurate translation, and the word translated "labor" is a very strong word; it means *intense toil,* or, *painful labor.* Do you know what it means to toil in prayer; to labor with painful toil in prayer? Oh, how easily most of us take our praying, how little heart we put into it, and how little it takes out of us, and how little it counts with God.

The mighty men of God, who throughout the centuries have wrought great things by prayer, are the men who have had much painful toil in prayer. Take, for example, David Brainerd, that physically feeble but spiritually mighty man of God. Trembling for years on the verge of consumption, from which he ultimately died at an early age, Brainerd felt led of God to labor among the North American Indians in the early days, in the primeval forests of Northern Pennsylvania, and sometimes of a winter night he would go out into the forest and kneel in the cold snow when it was a foot deep and so labor with God in prayer that he would be wringing wet with perspiration even out in the cold winter night hours. And God heard David Brainerd and sent such a mighty revival among the North American Indians as had never been heard of before, as indeed had never been dreamed about. And not only did God send in answer to David Brainerd's prayers this mighty revival among the North American Indians, but also in answer to David Brainerd's prayers he transformed David Brainerd's father-in-law, Jonathan Edwards, that mighty prince of metaphysicians, probably the mightiest thinker that America has ever produced (the only American metaphysician whose name is in the American Hall of Fame), into Jonathan Edwards the flaming evangelist. Edwards so preached on the subject of "Sinners in the Hands of an Angry God," in the church at Enfield, in the power of the Holy Spirit, that the strong men in the audience felt as he preached as if the very floor of the church were falling out and they were sinking into hell. They sprang to their feet and threw their arms around the pillars of the church and cried to God for mercy. Ah, that we had more men who could pray like David Brainerd, then we would have more men who could preach like Jonathan Edwards.

Speaking at a conference in New York State, I once used this illustration of David Brainerd. Dr. Park; the grandson and biographer of Jonathan Edwards, was in my audience and he came to me at the close and said, "I have always felt that there was something abnormal about David Brainerd."

I replied, "Dr. Park, it would be a good thing for

you and a good thing for me if we had a little more of that kind of abnormality."

Indeed it would; and it would be a good thing if many of us had that kind of so-called "abnormality" that bows a man down with intensity of longing for the power of God, that would make us pray in the way that David Brainerd prayed.

But a practical question arises at this point. How can we get this intense earnestness in prayer? The Bible answers the question plainly and simply. There are two ways of having earnestness in prayer—a right way and a wrong way. The wrong way is to work it up in the energy of the flesh. Have you never seen it done? A man kneels down by a chair to pray; he begins calmly and then he begins to work himself up and begins to shout and scream and pound the chair, and sometimes he spits foam; and he screams until your head is almost splitting with the loud uproar. That is the wrong way, that is false fire; that is the energy of the flesh, which is an abomination to God. If possible that is even worse than the careless, thoughtless prayers which I mentioned earlier.

There is a right way to obtain real, heart-stirring, heart-wringing, and God-moving earnestness in prayer. The right way the Bible tells us in Romans 8:26, 27 R.V., "And in like manner *the Spirit also helpeth our infirmity;* for we know not how to pray as we ought; but *the Spirit himself maketh intercession for us with groanings which cannot be uttered;* and he that searcheth the hearts knoweth what is the mind of the Spirit, because he maketh intercession for the saints according to the will of God." That is the right way—look to the Spirit to create the earnestness. The earnestness that counts with God is not the earnestness that you or I work up; it is the earnestness that the Holy Spirit creates in our hearts. Have you never gone to God in prayer with no earnestness in your prayer at all? It was just words, words, words, a mere matter of form; there seemed to be no real prayer in your heart. What do we do at such a time as that? Stop praying and wait until we feel more like praying? No. If there is ever a time when one needs to pray it is when he does not feel like praying. What *shall* we do? Be silent and look up to

God to send His Holy Spirit, according to His promise, to move your heart to prayer and to awaken and create real earnestness in your heart in prayer: and He will send Him and you will pray with intense earnestness, very likely "with groanings which cannot be uttered."

Oh, that is how we must pray if we would get what we ask in prayer. Pray with the intense earnestness that the Holy Ghost alone can inspire.

III. *Of the Church*

Now let us look briefly at another one of the four phrases, the phrase, *"of the church."* The prayer that God particularly delights to answer is united prayer. There is power in the prayer of a single individual, and the prayer of individuals has wrought great things, but there is far greater power in united prayer. Our Lord Jesus taught this same great truth in Matthew 18:19, 20, "Again I say unto you, *that if two of you shall agree* on earth as touching anything that they shall ask, *it shall be done for them of my Father who is in heaven."* God delights in the unity of His people, and He does everything in His power to promote that unity, and so He especially honors unity in prayer. There is power in the prayer of one true believer: there is far more power in the united prayer of two, and greater power in the united prayer of still more.

But *it must be real unity.* This comes out in the exact words our Lord uses; He says, "If two of you shall agree on earth *as touching anything* that they shall ask, it shall be done for them of my father who is in heaven." It is one of the most frequently misquoted and most constantly abused promises in the whole Bible. It is often quoted as if it read this way, "Again I say unto you, that if two of you shall agree on earth to ask anything, it shall be done for them of my Father who is in Heaven." But it actually reads, "Again I say unto you, that if two of you shall agree on earth *as touching* anything that they shall ask, it shall be done for them of my Father who is in Heaven." Someone may say, "I do not see any essential difference." Let me explain it to you. Someone else has a burden on his heart, he comes to you and asks you to unite with him in praying for this thing and you consent, and you both pray for it. Now you are "agreed" in praying, but you are not agreed at all *"as touching"* the thing that you ask. He asks for it because he intensely desires it; you ask for it simply because he asks you to ask for it. You are not at all agreed "as touching" the thing that you ask. But when God, by his Holy Spirit, puts the same burden on two hearts, and they thus in the unity of the Spirit pray for the same thing, there is no power on earth or in hell to keep them from getting it. Our Heavenly Father will do for them the thing that they ask.

IV. *"For Him"*

Now let us look at the fourth phrase, *"for him."* The prayer was definite prayer for a definite person; and that is the kind of prayer God answers, *definite prayer.* Oh, how general and vague many of our prayers are. They are pretty, they are charmingly phrased, but they ask no definite specific thing, and they get no definite, specific answer. When you pray to God, have a definite, clear-cut idea of just exactly what it is you want of God; and ask Him for that definite and specific thing; and, if you meet the other conditions of prevailing prayer, you will get that definite, specific thing which you asked. God's answer will be just as definite as your prayer.

In closing, let me call your attention to our dependence upon the Holy Spirit in all our praying, if we are to accomplish anything by our prayers. It is the Holy Spirit, as we saw in our study of the first phrase, who enables us to really pray *"unto God,"* who leads us into the presence of God and makes God real to us. It is the Holy Spirit again who gives us the intense earnestness in prayer that prevails with God. Still again it is the Holy Spirit who brings us into unity so that we know the power of really united prayer. And it is the Spirit who shows us the definite things for which we should definitely pray.

To sum it all up, the prayer that God answers is the prayer that is to God the Father, that is on the ground of the atoning blood of God the Son, and that is under the direction and in the power of God the Holy Spirit.

5

WHO CAN PRAY SO AS TO GET
WHAT THEY ASK?

*"And whatsoever we ask we receive of Him, because
we keep His commandments and do the things that are
pleasing in His sight."*—I JOHN 3:22.

In the last chapter we were studying together to find
what God tells us in His Word as to how to pray so as
to get what we ask. Now we take up the subject of
"Who can pray so as to get what they ask."

The impression that many people have is that all
the promises in the Word of God in regard to His
answering prayer are made to everyone, and that anyone can claim these promises; but this is far from the
truth. God's promises to answer prayer are made to
certain specified persons, and God is very careful in His
Word to tell us just who these persons are whose
prayers He promises to answer. One of the most common sources of misinterpretation of the Word of God
is the taking of promises that are made to one class of
people and applying them to an entirely different class.
Of course, when this is done, and people to whom the
promises were never made claim them, disappointment
is the inevitable result; they do not get what they ask
and they think that God's promise has failed. But God's
promise has not failed: someone has claimed the fulfillment of that promise who had no right to take the
promise as belonging to himself. God tells us in the
plainest possible words, words that any intelligent person can understand, just whose prayers it is He promises to answer.

76

One of the most definite and clearest descriptions to be found in the Bible of whose prayers God will answer, is found in John 3:22. Let me read it to you: "And *whatsoever we* ask we receive of him, *because we keep his commandments and do the things that are pleasing in his sight.*"

Have you ever noticed what a remarkable statement the apostle John makes in this verse? He says that whatever he asked of God he got, *"Whatsoever we ask* we receive of him." John here says he never asked one single thing of God but what he got that very thing he asked. How many of us could say that: *"Whatsoever* I ask of God I get"? Many of us doubtless could say *"Many* of the things I ask of God I get." Others could say *"some* of the things I ask of God I get"; and some of us would probably have to say, "I do not know that I have ever gotten one thing I asked of God." But John says *"Whatsoever I ask* of God I get." And then John goes on to tell us why he could say it, and by telling us *why he* could say it he tells us how we, too, can get into such a relation to God that we too can say, "whatsoever I ask I get."

I. *God Answers the Prayers of Those Who Keep His Commandments*

Whenever you find the word *"because"* in the Bible, or "wherefore" or "therefore," you should take careful notice for these words point out the reason of things. John here says that the reason God gave him whatever he asked was "because" he, and the others that he includes with himself in the word "we," *keep His commandments* and *do the things that are pleasing in His sight.* There are two parts to John's description of those whose prayers God always answers.

The first part of the description is, "We keep His commandments." *God hears the prayers of those who "keep His commandments," that is, those who study His Word each day to find out what His will is, and who, when they discover what His will is, do it every time they find it.* God demands reciprocity: He demands that we listen to His Word before He listens to our prayers. If we have a sharp ear for God's commandments, then God will have a sharp ear for our petitions; but if we turn a deaf ear to one of God's commandments, God will turn a deaf ear to every one of our petitions. If we do the things that God bids us to do, then God will do the things that we ask Him to do; but if we do not pay close attention to God's Word, God will pay no attention whatever to our prayers. To put it all in a single sentence: If we wish God to answer our prayers, we must study God's Word diligently each day, to find out what the will of God is, and do that will *every time* we find it.

Here we touch upon one of the most common reasons why prayers are not answered: those who pray are neglecting the study of the Word of God, or they are not studying it for the particular purpose of finding out what God's will is for them, or else they are not doing that will every time they find it out. In my first pastorate there was a lady who was a constant attendant upon the services of the church, but who was not a member of the church. She was one of the most intelligent women in the community. One day someone told me that this lady had formerly been a member of the church of which I was pastor. So one Sunday morning, as I was walking home from church, I walked along with this lady, who lived on the same street as I. When we reached my front gate and I was about to turn in, I said to her, "They tell me you were formerly a member of this church of which I am pastor."

She replied, "Yes, I was."

"Well," I said, "why are you not a member now?"

She answered, "Because I do not believe the Bible."

I said, "Do not believe the Bible?"

"No," she said, "I do not believe the Bible."

I asked, "Why do you not believe the Bible?"

She replied, "Because I have tried its promises and found them untrue."

I said, "Will you tell me one single promise in the Word of God that you ever tried and found untrue?"

She said, "Does it not say somewhere in the Bible that whatsoever things ye desire when ye pray, believe that ye receive them and ye shall have them?"

I said, "It says something that sounds a good deal like that."

She said, "My husband was very ill. I prayed for his recovery and I fully believed God would raise him up, but he died. Did not the promise fail?"

"No, not at all," I said.

"What?" she exclaimed, "the promise did not fail?"

"No," I replied, "the promise did not fail."

"But," she said, "does it not say that what things soever ye desire when ye pray, believe that ye receive them and ye shall have them?"

I said, "It says something that sounds a good deal like that."

"Just what does it say?"

I replied, "It says, 'whatsoever things *ye* desire when ye pray, believe that ye receive them and *ye* shall have them.' Are you one of the 'Ye's'?"

She asked, "What do you mean?"

I replied, "Are you one of the people to whom this promise is made?"

"Why," she exclaimed, "isn't it made to every professing Christian?"

I replied, "Certainly not. God defines very clearly in His Word just to whom His promises to answer prayer are made."

"I would like to see God's definition," she said.

I said, "Let me show it to you," and I opened my Bible to I John 3:22, and read, "Whatsoever *we* ask *we* receive of him, because *we keep his commandments* and do the things that are pleasing to his sight." Then I said, "That is God's definition of the *'we's'* and the *'ye's'* whose prayers God promises to answer; those who 'keep His commandments and do the things that are pleasing in His sight.' Were you keeping His commandments? Were you doing the things that are pleasing in His sight? Were you living for the glory of God in everything?"

"No," she said, "I certainly was not."

"Then," I said, "the promise was not made to you, was it?"

"No," she said, "it was not."

"Then it did not fail?"

"No, it did not." She saw her error and came back to God and became one of the most active and most useful members of that church.

There are a multitude of men and women just like that woman: they take a promise that is made to someone else and apply it to themselves, and of course it fails. Are you one of the *ye's?* That is, are you studying the Word of God every day of your life, earnestly and carefully, to find out what is God's will for you, and are you doing it every time you find it? If so, you are on praying ground and belong to the class whose prayers God will answer and give you what you ask. If not, you do not belong to the class whose prayers God promises to answer.

I had another illustration of this same thing in our church in Chicago. I had in my church two women, one the mistress, the other the maid. The mistress was an earnest and intelligent Christian. One night at the close of a meeting the maid came to me and said, "Miss W—— (that is, her mistress), thinks, Mr. Torrey, that I ought to have a talk with you."

"Why, Jennie, does Miss W—— think that you ought to have a talk with me?"

"Because I am in great perplexity."

I said, "What are you perplexed about?"

She replied, "I am perplexed because God does not answer my prayers."

"Oh," I said, "there is nothing to be surprised about in that. Does God anywhere promise to answer your prayers? God does tell us very plainly in His Word whose prayers He will answer." Then I quoted again I John 3:22: "Whatsoever *we* ask *we* receive of him, *because we keep his commandments* and do the things that are pleasing in his sight."

"Now, Jennie," I said, "does that describe you? Are you studying the Word of God every day of your life to find out what God wishes you to do, and do you do it every time you find it?"

"No," she replied, "I do not."

"Then," I said, "there is nothing mysterious, is there, about God's not answering your prayers?"

"No," she said, "there is not."

I put the same question to each one of you. Are you studying the Word of God every day of your life to find out what the will of God is, and doing it every time you find it? If you are, as I have said, you are on praying ground, and God will heed your prayers and give you the things that you ask of Him; but if you are neglecting the study of the Word of God, to find out what His will is, or failing to do that will every time that you discover it, then you have no right whatever to expect God to answer your prayers. He does not promise to do so. Indeed, He distinctly says in His Word that He will not.

Now, you may go right through your Bible and you will find, in regard to every one of the great promises of God to answer our prayers, that this same thought comes out, in the connection in which the promise is found. Take, for example, that wonderful promise of Jesus Christ to answer prayer, which is so often quoted and is so familar to us all—John 14:13-14, "And *whatsoever ye* shall ask in my name, *that* will I do, that the Father may be glorified in the Son. If *ye* shall ask anything in my name I will do it." Now, most people, when they quote this promise, stop there, and therefore get the impression that if *anyone* asks anything in Christ's name, Jesus Christ offers to do it. But Jesus Christ did not stop there, He went on. Look at it again:

"And whatsoever ye shall ask in my name, that will I do, that the Father may be glorified in the Son. If ye ask anything in my name, I will do it. If ye love me, *keep my commandments,* (or, as the Revised Version reads, 'If ye love me ye will *keep my commandments'*), and I will pray the Father and he will give you another Comforter, that he may abide with you forever, even the Spirit of Truth: Whom the world cannot receive, because it seeth him not, neither knoweth him, but ye know him, for he dwelleth with you, and shall be in you."

In other words, Jesus Christ said to His disciples that if they had that love to Him that led them to keep His commandments (that is, to study His Word and find out what His commandments were, and did them every time they discovered them) that He would pray the Father, and the Father, in answer to His prayers, would give *them* the Holy Spirit, and the Holy Spirit would guide *them* in their prayers, so that they would pray "according to the will of God," and that whatsoever *they* (they who keep His commandments and were therefore led by the Holy Spirit) should ask in His Name, that He would do.

Turn to another familiar promise—one of the most remarkable promises in the whole Bible regarding God's answering prayer—John 15:9, "If ye abide in me, and *my words abide in you,* ye shall ask what ye will, and it shall be done unto you." This verse is constantly quoted as if it read "If ye abide in me, ye shall ask what ye will and it shall be done unto you," but it does not so read. You have left out one of the most important clauses in the verse. Let me read it again as it really reads: "If ye abide in me, *and my words abide in you,* ye shall ask what ye will and it shall be done unto you." So the Lord Jesus tells us that it is not only necessary that we abide in Him, but that *His words abide in us,* if we are to ask so as to get what we ask.

Now, in order that Christ's words may abide in us, we must study these words, must we not? Unless we get them in us, they certainly cannot stay in us, and we certainly cannot get Christ's words in us unless we study them diligently.

But it is not enough to get Christ's words in us: His words must *"abide"* in us, that is, *"stay"* in us, and there is only one possible way in which Christ's words can stay in us, and that is by our diligently obeying them. Three verses further down in this same chapter Jesus says again, "If ye *keep my commandments,* ye *shall abide* in my love, even as *I have kept my Father's commandments* and *abide* in His love." So you can go right straight through your Bible and you will find that every promise of God to answer our prayers is made to those who diligently study His Word that they may know His will, and who always obey His will every time they find it. Are you greatly perplexed as to why God does not give you the things you ask? There is no mystery at all about it; you are not studying God's Word to find out His will for you, or else you are not doing it every time you find it. You are doing it in many instances, but there is some particular thing you are not doing that you know God wishes you to do, and there is not the slightest reason why you should expect God to answer your prayers.

82

II. *God Answers Prayers of Those Who Do the Things That Are Pleasing in His sight*

But it is not enough that we keep His commandments. There is something further than that in the verse that we are studying. Let me read it to you again. I John 3:22—"And *whatsoever we ask* we receive of him, because we keep his commandments, *and* [please notice that *and;* 'and' is a little word but a very important word] *do those things that are pleasing in his sight.*" It is not enough that we do the things that God specifically commands us to do; in addition to that, we must "do the things that are pleasing in his sight," even though He has not commanded us to do them. There are many things that it would please God for us to do that He does not specifically command us to do.

The idea that many people have of God's government is this: that God is a great moral Governor, and that He lays down a lot of laws for us to obey: thou shalt do this, and thou shalt do this, and thou shalt do this, and thou shalt not do this, and thou shalt not do this, and thou shalt not do this; and that the whole of Christian duty lies in our doing the things that God specifically tells us to do, and leaving undone the things that God specifically tells us not to do. What a strange idea of God's government! God is not a mere moral governor. He is that, but He is far more than that; something infinitely better than that. God is our Father. That is the thought that lies at the very foundation of the Bible doctrine of prayer—the thought of the Fatherhood of God. And all these apparently philosophical and learned arguments that men bring against the doctrine of God's answering prayer, from "the uniformity of law," and from "the established course of things in nature and in providence," are all utterly foolish, and really unphilosophical (for all their ostentatious parade of being profoundly scientific and philosophical), because they lose sight of the great fundamental truth about God that lies at the very foundation of the Bible doctrine that God answers prayer—the truth that God is not merely a Creator and the Governor of the physical universe and the moral universe, but that God is our Father.

Now, how does a father govern his children? Does he lay down a lot of laws—thou shalt do this, and thou shalt do this, and thou shalt do this, and thou shalt not do this, and thou shalt not do this, and thou shalt not do this? Does he rest content when his children do the things that he specifically tells them to do, and leave undone the things he specifically tells them not to do? No, not if he is a wise father. If he is a wise father he will lay down some rules for the conduct of his children, which he, because of superior knowledge, knows to be wise. But those rules will not be so very many, and certainly he will not be content if his children simply obey those rules. No, the wise father expects his children to get thoroughly acquainted with him, so that they know what pleases him instinctively and, when they know what pleases him, do it *without waiting to be told.*

Take my own government of my children, and my wife's government of our children. Did we lay down a lot of laws for our children to follow, as to what they should do and what they should not do? No, certainly not. We did lay down a few principles of action, which we, in our superior wisdom, knew to be best for our children, and we did not always explain to our children why we laid down these laws for we wished our children to learn obedience to authority. In much of the home life of America today, and in much of the school life, and in much of our national life, we have entirely lost sight of the great and wholesome principle of *authority,* and some of our modern would-be educators tell us that we ought to explain everything that we command our children to do, in the home or in the school, and that we ought to let our children "follow out their own individuality," and "not enslave them by parental or school authority."

That is one of the most dangerous principles in modern teaching. By it we are training a lot of rebels— rebels in the home, rebels in the schools, and afterwards rebels in society and in civil government. If there is anything the present generation needs to learn, and that we, who are in authority of one kind or another, need to teach our children, it is the principle of rightful authority: the authority of the parent in the home, the authority of teachers in schools, and the authority of civil rulers in our government. So our children were taught to obey when they were told to do anything, *without asking "why."* And if either their mother or their father had told our children to do anything, and they had not done it, we would not have known what to make of it; or if we had told them not to do anything and they had done it, we would not have known what to make of that. I cannot recall an instance in many years in which our children disobeyed us in a single matter.

But we were not satisfied with that. Over and above the few rules we laid down for the guidance of our children, we expected our children to become thoroughly acquainted with us, so that they would know instinctively what would please their father or their mother, and, when they knew it, do it without waiting to be told. We should have been much grieved if our children had only done the things that pleased us when they were specifically told to do them.

Now, when we thus are carefully considering in all our actions and in all our decisions as to our conduct, what would please God and what would displease God, and do every time the things we think would please Him, and refuse to do, every time, the things we think would displease Him, even though He has not specifically told us to do the one, or leave undone the other, then God will listen to our prayers. If we always study to "do the things that are pleasing in His sight," He will always study to do the things that please us, and, therefore, grant our requests. Are you always, in all your decisions, carefully considering what would please or displease God, and doing every time the things that you think would please Him, and leaving undone every time the things you think would displease Him, whether He has told you to do the one or not to do the other, or not?

Here we find a very simple way of deciding the questions that are perplexing so many young Christians today, yes, and older Christians, too: for example, the question, "Shall Christians go to the theatre," or "Shall

Christians dance," or "Shall Christians play cards," or "Shall Christians go to the movies?" etc., etc. Now the way a great many people seek to decide those questions is this. They ask, "Does God anywhere say in His Word, 'Thou shalt not go to the theatre'; 'Thou shalt not dance'; 'Thou shalt not play cards'?" That is not the question. If you were a real loyal child of God you would not ask that question. The question is, "Will it please my Father? Will it please God?"

Take, for example, the question of the theatre. If I thought it would please God for me to go to the theatre, more than for me to stay away, I would go, no matter what anyone else might think of it, or what anyone else might do. But if I thought it would please God for me to stay away more than for me to go, I would stay away no matter who else went.

When I lived in Chicago I frequently had sent to me complimentary tickets from different theatres, especially from one of the highest class theatres, and with the tickets oftentimes would come a note saying that the play was of a very high moral character, and that Bishop So and So, in some city, or Dr. So and So, highly approved of it and had gone to the play, and that they would be highly complimented if I would occupy a box at the play. Now, I could not be caught by any such chaff as that. It made no difference to me what Bishop or Doctor So and So had done. The only question with me was, will it please God better for me to go than for me to stay away? And had I thought that it would please God better for me to go than for me to stay away, I would have gone, whether Bishop So and So had gone or not. But if, on the other hand, I had thought it would please God better for me to stay away, I would have stayed away, even though every bishop and every minister in Chicago had gone.

Each one of us must decide these questions for ourselves. No one of us can be a conscience for someone else. But they are not at all difficult to decide if we decide them on this Bible basis of doing the things that would please our Father, and leaving undone the things that would not please Him.

Take, for example, the theatre. Does it please God for a child of His to attend the theatre? Now, there are certain things that we all know about the theatre, or that we may easily learn if we do not already know them. We all know there is a great difference between the plays that are put on the stage. Some of them are of a high moral character and the natural effect of them would be uplifting. Others are not morally so good, and others are as vile as the theatrical people dare make them. Then we know, too, that there is a great difference between actors and actors, and between actresses and actresses. We know that some actors and actresses try to maintain a high moral standard, and that others are among the most corrupt members of modern society. We know that some actresses go on the stage with lofty moral ideals, and that other actresses have no moral ideals at all. "Well, then," someone may say, "the way to decide it is this: go to those plays, and only to those plays, where the play itself is of a high, elevating moral character, and where all the actors and actresses are men and women who are trying to maintain high moral ideals."

Well, if you decided it in that way, you would not go to many plays. But the question is not quite that simple. The theatre is an institution, and we must judge it as an institution, judge it as it really exists today. It is possible to imagine a stage of the purest and loftiest character, and to imagine plays that would be among the most elevating of all the influences in society; but the question is not of the stage, and the plays, as we can imagine them, but of the stage as it actually exists today.

Now, there are certain things that all of us who have studied the problem at all thoroughly, know about the stage as it exists today. We know that the influence of the stage upon the men and women who perform upon it is of a most demoralizing character. We know that many a woman has gone on the stage with a determination to maintain the highest moral ideals, and that they have all found out, after they have been on the stage a while, that they must do one of two things—they must either lower their flag, or else quit the stage. Some have quit the stage. Others have lowered their flag.

Clement Scott, who was the leading dramatic critic of his day in England, and whose whole life was given to dramatic criticism, said some years ago in a leading London paper, over his own name, that it was practically impossible for any woman to remain on the stage and retain her womanly modesty. This statement of his naturally aroused great excitement among theatrical people, and great indignation, and by threats of one kind and another they compelled Clement Scott to say that he was sorry that he made the statement, but they could never make him say that it was not true.

When Mr. Alexander and I were holding meetings in London, Herbert Beerbohm Tree, who stood at the top of the dramatic profession of that day, and who was afterwards knighted by the king because of his prominence and rare gifts, came down to see me at my lodgings, with one of the leading newspaper men of London, to convince me that I was wrong in my attitude toward the stage. We had a long conversation. I invited Mr. Alexander in to listen to the conversation and he took part in it. In that conversation both Mr. Alexander and myself put some very direct questions to Beerbohm Tree, and he answered them frankly; and the admissions that he made (not, of course, regarding any matter in his own moral conduct, but regarding what was necessary to be done in the conduct of the stage), made me think worse of the theatre than I ever had before.

When I was holding meetings in the big armory in Cleveland, Ohio, a theatrical manager called upon me at my hotel and he said, "I demand the right to defend the stage from your platform."

I asked, "Why?"

He said, "Because you are doing a great profession a great wrong. I was in Philadelphia when you held your meetings there, and we theatrical managers got together while you were there, and we agreed together that your meetings cost the theatres of Philadelphia fifty thousand dollars."

I replied, "That is one of the best things I have ever heard about our meetings in Philadelphia. Now," I said, "what do you want to say?"

He said, "I want to defend the stage."

"Well," I said, "the Paris *Figaro* has said that it is wrong to judge actresses by the same moral canons that

88

we judge other women; for what would be wrong in other women would be right in actresses, for it is a part of their art."

"Well," he said, "that is just what I believe."

"Well," I said, "that is worse than anything I have ever said about the theatre."

While I was in that same city of Cleveland, one of the most highly respected actors was performing with his troupe in the city at that time. It was a famous troupe, known on both sides of the water, and of high repute. One of the leading ladies in the troupe came under the influence of our meetings, and in conversation with my private secretary, another woman told her what was practically required of any woman who hoped to become a star. When it was reported to me, I could not help but feel that I would rather see a daughter of my own in her coffin than to see her on the stage. Is God pleased when a child of His patronizes an institution like that, which has such an influence upon the women who perform on the stage?

When Mr. Alexander and I were holding meetings in London, and I had said some pretty plain things about the stage in our meetings in the Royal Albert Hall, I received a letter from a man who was managing at that time more than thirty theatres in London. He wrote me saying, "I am the manager of more than thirty theatres in London at the present time, but I want to write you that every word you have said about the stage is true. I wish I were not in the business, but I am. Nevertheless, what you say is true." A number of people quite prominently connected with the stage gave up that work during our meetings in London.

How about the dance? Ought a Christian to dance? The answer to that question is found in the other question, Will it please God? Is God better pleased when a child of His dances, or when His child refuses to dance? Now, there are certain things that we all know about the dance. First of all, we know that a familiarity of contact is permitted between the sexes in the modern dance that is nowhere else permitted in decent society. How is it any better in the dance than it is elsewhere?

When I was in Balarat, Australia, I said some pretty

plain things about the dance, which led to a good many of the dancers giving up the dance, and to the breaking up of a prominent dancing club in the city. Some months afterward I was crossing over from Tasmania to Australia, and a fellow passenger on the boat was a lawyer from Balarat. This lawyer came to me and said, "Are you not Dr. Torrey?"

"Yes."

"Well, I do not think you were fair to the dancers of Balarat."

"What did I say that was not true?"

He replied, "I simply think you were not fair."

"Yes, but will you state one single thing that was not true?"

He said, "I simply think you were not fair."

"Now, see here," I said, "do you dance?"

"Yes."

"Are you a married man?"

"Yes."

"Does your wife dance?"

"Yes."

"Well, tell me, if you should see your wife in the same attitude toward some other man than yourself, at any other place than the ballroom, that she takes in the ballroom, what would you do?"

He replied, "There would be trouble."

I said, "Will you please tell me how it is any better in the ballroom, to the strains of seductive music, than anywhere else? Now, tell me another thing. Do you not know that in every class of society, even the most select, there are some men who are moral lepers?"

He replied, "Of course we all know, Dr. Torrey, that in every class of society there are men who are corrupt."

"And your wife dances with those men?"

"Well," he said, "she does not know their character."

"You are willing," I said, "that your wife should be in the embrace of some other man who is a moral leper, simply because she does not know his character?"

He made no reply. What reply could be made?

Now, I do not believe for one single moment that every woman who dances has evil thoughts. I think

90

that some of the girls who dance are sweet, innocent, pure-minded girls; but, if they knew the thoughts that were in the minds of the men with whom they dance, they would never go on the floor again. Three young men came to me in an eastern college town and said to me. "Dr. Torrey, what have you got against the dance?"

I replied, "Do you dance?"

"Yes."

"Are you Christians?"

"Yes."

"Will you please tell me what your thoughts are when you dance?"

They said, "Our thoughts are all right if we dance with a pure girl."

I said, "Do you dance with any other kind?"

"Well," they said, "you know, Dr. Torrey, that there are some girls that are not what they ought to be."

"And," I said, "you dance with them?"

"Yes."

"Well, you have answered your own question."

It is a well-known fact, proven by many a test, that the select dance is the greatest feeder of, and auxiliary to, the most awful institution that exists in civilized society today. Oh! if pure women could only know where many of the young men who dance with them go immediately after the dance is over, if I could only tell you things that I know personally, not that I have read in books but that have come under my own personal observation, regarding the effect of the select dance, among what are called the better classes of society, there is not a self-respecting woman who would go on the floor again.

But what about cards? Ought a Christian to play cards? Now, I frankly admit that I do not think the case against the cards is as clear as is the case against the theatre or the dance; but it is clear enough. Everyone who has studied the matter knows that cards are the gambler's darling weapon. We know, also, that pretty much every gambler took the first lessons that led him to the gaming table, at the quiet family card table. I have never known a single reformed gambler in my life (and I have known many of them) who did not hate the cards as he hated poison. Why? Because he knew that the cards were the secret of his own downfall.

When we were holding meetings in Nashville, Tennessee, my wife went out to one of the penal institutions near Nashville, and there she learned of a man who was serving a life sentence for murder, because he had shot a man at the gaming table. He said that he took his first step in that direction by tallying for his mother as she played cards with her friends.

Some years ago a Y.M.C.A. secretary in Ohio was going to the State penitentiary to make a visit upon some of the prisoners. Before he left, a lady came to him and asked, "Are you going to visit the prisoners?"

He said, "Yes."

She said, "I have a son in that prison. Will you take him this Bible for me, and say that his mother sent it to him?"

The Y.M.C.A. secretary consented. When he reached the prison he asked for this young man. The young man was brought in. He started to hand him the Bible saying, "Your mother sent you this Bible."

The prisoner looked at him and said, "Did my mother send me that Bible?"

"Yes."

"Well," he said, "you can take it right back to my mother. I do not want my mother's Bible. If my mother had not taught me to play cards, I would not be here today. I do not want my mother's Bible. Take it back to her."

I knew of a family where the father and mother tried to make home so pleasant for their three sons that they would not wish to go anywhere else of a night; and they did make their home pleasant—the pleasantest place in the whole community, and the sons were perfectly contented to spend their nights at home. Among other things, to amuse their children, this father and mother played cards with them. Of the three sons, one did not have a taste for the cards. He was not better than the other two. His tastes simply ran in another direction. The other two played cards at home. Now this theory of making home so pleasant would have been all right, if young men were always to stay at home, but the time comes for young men to leave home. These three young men left home, and the two who had learned to play cards at home, with their Christian father and mother, both became gamblers.

Major Cole, the evangelist, was once holding meetings in an Arkansas city. At one of the meetings, in the Presbyterian church, a disreputable looking man came in and took a seat over on the right-hand side of the church. When the meeting was opened for testimonies, this moral derelict arose in his place, looked around the church, and said, "All this looks very familiar to me. When I was a boy I attended this church. My father was an elder in this church. This is our old pew, where I am standing. There were seven of us boys who were in a Sunday school class. Our teacher was a very kind lady. She not only taught us the Bible on Sundays, but invited us to her house on Saturday afternoons to teach us the Bible, and to play games with us. One day after we had been going there a while, she brought out a pack of cards and showed us tricks with the cards. Later we played games with the cards. We soon wanted more cards, and asked the teacher if she would not give us less Bible and more cards. But we did not get enough cards there, so we left Sunday school and spent our Sunday afternoons in a cotton press, playing cards.

"There were seven members in the class. Two of those members have already been hanged; two are in state prisons at the present time; I have lost track of one; the sixth member of the class is at present a fugitive from justice, and if the authorities knew where he was he would be under arrest; and I am the seventh member of that class, and if the authorities knew where I was I would be under arrest." Just then a lady dressed in black, in the back of the church, sprang to her feet, came running down the aisle with her hands flung in the air, and crying, "Oh, my God, and I am that teacher," she fell at his feet as though she were dead. They thought for a while that she was dead. I would not like to have been that teacher. Oh! fathers and mothers, happy is the young man or young woman who goes out into the world not knowing one card from another, and fully instructed in the peril there is in the cards. And if any of you parents have a pack of cards in your home, I advise you to burn it up as soon as you get home.

Well, how about the movies? I do not need to dwell upon that. The movies are worse than the theatre ever dreamed of being, immeasurably worse. The stage, at its worst, was never so occupied with the most open depiction of degrading sin as are the movies today, and the character of movie actors and actresses is notorious. I do not mean to say for one single moment that every movie actress is immoral. I know better. One of the most modest, and sweetest Christian young women I ever knew, who is now a minister's wife, and a beautiful Christian mother, was, when I first became acquainted with her, a movie actress. And I do not question that there are others like her. But the lives of movie actors and actresses, taken as a whole, are full of the most terrible temptations, and many have yielded to those temptations. Movie plays as they exist today (I am not talking about educational movies, although some that are paraded as educational are among the vilest plays there are) are, for the most part, one of the greatest menaces that exist to the young life of our country, and also to pure family life. Is God pleased when a child of His patronizes a movie, when it is what we all know it is today?

There are many other things which I might mention, but this is enough to illustrate the principle. But some one will ask, "Dr. Torrey, do you mean to say that dancing, theatre-going, card-playing, and going to the movies, is a sin, in the sense that stealing is a sin, and adultery is a sin, and murder is a sin, and gossiping is a sin, and slandering your neighbors is a sin?" No, I do not say that. "Then," you ask, "Wherein is the harm in it?" Right here: our indulging in these things does not please God, and therefore they rob prayer of power; and I want every ounce of power in prayer that I can have, and if there is anything, no matter how innocent it may be in itself, or however much can be said in defense of it, that robs prayer of power, I am going to give it up.

Remember, in all that I am saying I am not legislating for the world. If it were in my power to pass a law that there should be no more dancing, no more card-playing, no more theatres, no more movies, I would not pass it. I would not believe in it. No, I am not legislating at all for the unsaved about these matters, or other matters. I am simply trying to tell men and women who profess to be Christians how to get the most out of your Christian life, and, in particular at this time, how to have power in prayer. And, beyond an honest question, these things rob prayer of power. The Christian who dances, or goes to the theatre, or plays cards, or attends the movies, or does many other things which are not pleasing to God, cannot be a man or woman of power in prayer.

To sum up all we have said: the ones who can pray so that God will hear their prayers, and give them whatever they ask, are those who study the Word of God every day of their lives to find out what the will of God is, and do it every time they find it, and who further than that, make it their study to get thoroughly acquainted with God, so that they know instinctively what will please God and what will displease God, and in every action of their lives seek to do the thing that pleases God, whether it please men or not, and not to do the thing that displeases God, no matter who else may do it. Oh! that we all might enter into the wonderful place of privilege described in our text: "*Whatsoever we* ask *we receive of him, because we keep his commandments, and do the things that are pleasing in his sight.*"

6

PRAYING IN THE NAME OF JESUS CHRIST

"And whatsoever ye shall ask in my name, that will I do, that the Father may be glorified in the Son. If ye shall ask anything in my name, that will I do."—JOHN 14:13, 14.

This is one of the most familiar, most wonderful, and at the same time most commonly misunderstood promises in the Bible regarding God's willingness to answer prayer.

Here our Lord Jesus Christ Himself tells us that if a certain class of people pray in a certain way, He will give them the very thing that they ask. Look at the promise again. "Whatsoever *ye* shall ask *in my name, that* will I do, that the Father may be glorified in the Son. If *ye* shall ask anything *in my name, that* will I do." These words are plain, simple, positive, very precious and cheering. They tell us there are certain people who can get from God anything that they ask for, if only they will ask for it in a certain way.

There is a doctrine regarding prayer that is very common in our day. It is this: "If we pray, our praying will do much good in many ways. We may not get the very thing that we ask, but we will get something, something just as good as that which we ask, or perhaps something far better than what we ask." I do not doubt that there is a measure of truth in that doctrine. It is a good thing sometimes that some of us do not get what we ask for; we are so careless, and so thoughtless, and so hasty, and so little under the control of the Holy

96

Spirit when we pray, that it is oftentimes a good thing for us, and a good thing for others, that we do not get the very thing that we ask. It would be a great misfortune if some of us got some of the things that we ask of God. But while there is a certain measure of truth in that doctrine, it is not the doctrine of prayer taught in the Bible. The doctrine of prayer taught in the Bible is, that there are certain people who can pray in a certain way and who will get not merely some good thing, or something just as good as what they ask, or something even better than what they ask, but *they will get the very thing that they ask.* "*Whatsoever* ye shall ask in my name, *that* will I do, that the Father may be glorified in the Son. If ye shall ask *anything* in my name, *that* will I do." There are two things to notice about this promise: First, *who* it is to whom the promise is made, who it is that can ask in the name of the Lord Jesus and get the very thing they ask; second, *how* these persons must pray to get what they ask.

I. *To Whom the Promise Is Made*

First of all, notice to whom this promise is made. One of the most common sources of misinterpretation of the Bible is the applying of promises that are made to a certain clearly defined class of people to whom the promises were never made. God does not promise to answer the prayers of everyone; indeed, He tells us plainly that there are people to whose prayers He will pay no attention whatever. In the case of the present promise we are told very definitely in the context, in what goes before and what comes after the promise, just who it is whose prayers God will answer, if they are offered in a certain way. Who are the people to whom God says through His Son Jesus Christ, "Whatsoever *ye* shall ask in my name, that will I do"? They are clearly described in verse twelve, the verse that immediately precedes, and verses fifteen and seventeen, the verses that immediately follow the promise.

1. First of all, then, look at verse twelve, "Verily, verily, I say unto you, *He that believeth on me,* the works that I do shall he do also; and greater works than these shall he do; because I go unto the Father." And

97

then our Lord goes on to say, "And whatsoever *ye* [that is, *ye that believe on the Son,* as just defined] shall ask in my name, that will I do." The promise then is made, first of all, *to those who believe upon Jesus Christ.* Notice that it is not made to those who believe *about* Jesus Christ, but those who believe *on* Jesus Christ. People are constantly confusing in their own minds two entirely different things, believing about Jesus Christ and believing on Jesus Christ. God does not promise to answer the prayers of those who merely believe *about* Jesus Christ even though their faith is perfectly and rigidly orthodox. He does promise to answer the prayers of those who believe *on* Jesus Christ. A person may believe perfectly correctly about Jesus Christ, and yet not believe on Him at all. The devil himself believes *about* Jesus Christ, and is doubt-less perfectly orthodox; he knows more about Jesus Christ as He really is than we do, but the devil certain-ly does not believe *on* Jesus Christ. There are many today who, because their view of Jesus Christ is per-fectly orthodox, imagine that they believe on Jesus Christ. But that does not follow at all.

What does it mean to believe on Jesus Christ? *To believe on Jesus Christ means to put our personal confidence in Jesus Christ as what He claims to be, and to accept Him to be to ourselves what He offers Him-self to be to us.* It means for us to accept Him as our Savior, as the one who bore our sins in His own body upon the cross, and to trust God to forgive us because Jesus Christ died in our place, and also to accept Him as our Lord and Master to whom we surrender the absolute control of our lives. This we are told in so many words in the first chapter of this same Book, in the twelfth verse: "But as many as *received him* to them gave he the right to become children of God, *even to them that believe on* his name."

Nowhere in the whole Bible does God promise to hear the prayers of people who do not believe on Jesus Christ, i. e., the prayers of people who are not united to Jesus Christ by a living faith in Himself as their Savior, and as their Lord. I do not say that God never answers the prayers of those who are not believers on Jesus Christ. I believe that He sometimes does. He answered

98

some of my prayers before I was, in the Bible sense, a believer on Him, but He does not promise to do it. His doing it belongs to what the old theologians used to call so aptly "the uncovenanted mercies of God." He *promises most plainly and most positively to answer the prayers of those who believe on Jesus Christ, but never does He promise to answer the prayers of those who do not believe on Jesus Christ.* Anyone who does not believe on Jesus Christ has no right whatever to expect God to answer his prayers, and he has no cause whatever to complain that the promises of God are not true because He does not answer his prayers. There are many people who say they know that God does not answer prayer, because He has never answered their prayers, and they have tried it time and time again. But that is no proof whatever that God does not answer prayer, for God has never promised to answer *their* prayers.

That is one of the many good things about believing on Jesus Christ, it puts us on praying ground, it puts us in the place where we may go to God in every time of need and get from Him the very thing that we need and ask for. I would rather be on praying ground, rather be in such a relation to God that He can and will answer my prayers, than to have the combined wealth of a hundred Rockefellers. Times will come in the life of every one of us sooner or later when no earthly friend can help us, and no amount of wealth can help us; but the time will never come when God cannot help us and deliver us completely. This important question, therefore, confronts every one of us, "Do I believe on Jesus Christ?" Not do I believe about Him, but do I believe on Him? If you do not, there is but one wise thing to do. There is but one thing to do that has even the slightest semblance of intelligence; and that is, to believe on Jesus Christ right now. Put your confidence in Him as your Savior right now, and look to God to forgive your sins right now because Jesus Christ died in your place, and also put your confidence in Him right now as your Lord and Master to whom you surrender the entire control of your thoughts and your life and your conduct, right now.

2. But this is not all of the description of those

99

whose prayers God promises to answer. The rest of the description of this fortunate class we find in the fifteenth verse, the verse that follows the promise. *"If ye love me ye will keep my commandments."* The promise then is made to those who believe on Jesus Christ and who love Him with that genuine love that leads them to keep His commandments. Of course, to keep His commandments we must know them, and to know them we must study His Word, in which He has revealed His will to us. So we see that *the promise is made to those who study the Word of God each day of their lives that they may know what God's will is regarding their conduct, and who, when they discover it, do it every time.* This brings us to just where we were when we were studying I John 3:22: "And whatsoever we ask we receive of him, *because we keep his commandments* and do the things that are pleasing in his sight."

There is not a promise in the whole Book of God that God will hear and answer the prayers of a disobedient child. If we are to expect God to listen to us when we pray to Him, we must first of all listen to God when He speaks to us in His Word. We must obey God every time He commands and then (and only then) He will hear every time we pray. We must study His Word each day of our lives that we may find out what His will is, and when we find it do it every time. Then, and only then, are we on praying ground.

To sum it all up, then, *The promise of God to give to a certain class of people whatever they ask in a certain way, is made to those who are united to Him by a living faith, and an obedient love, to them and to them alone.* Someone may wish to ask, "Which is more important in the prayer life, that we have a living faith in Jesus Christ or an obedient love to Jesus Christ?" The answer is simple. You cannot have one without the other. If you have a living faith in Jesus Christ, it will lead inevitably to an obedient love to Jesus Christ. Paul states this clearly in Galatians 5:6: "For in Christ Jesus neither circumcision availeth anything, nor uncircumcision; *but faith which worketh by love."* On the other hand, you will never love Jesus Christ until you begin by believing in His love to you. We begin by believing
100

in His love to us and end by loving Him. Or, as John puts it, in I John 4:19: "We love him, *because he first loved us.*" There are many people who are trying to love God as a matter of duty, but no one ever succeeds in that attempt. Of course, we *ought* to love God, for He is infinitely worthy of our love. We ought to love Him because of His moral perfection, and because He is the infinite One and our Creator; but no one ever did love Him for that reason nor ever will or ever can. Here is where the Unitarians, under the leadership of Channing and other great intellectual leaders of his day, made their mistake. They tried to love God as a matter of duty. We never can and never will. But if we will first of all just put our trust in His wonderful love to us, vile and worthless sinners, we will soon find ourselves loving Him without an effort. Love to God is the inevitable outcome of our believing in His love to us.

One day in London a little girl came to Mark Guy Pearse, the great English preacher, and looked up wistfully into his face and said, "Mr. Pearse, I don't love Jesus. I wish I did love Jesus, but I don't love Jesus. Won't you please tell me how to love Jesus?" And the great preacher looked down into those eager eyes and said to her, "Little girl, as you go home today keep saying to yourself, 'Jesus loves me. Jesus loves me. Jesus loves me.' And when you come back next Sunday I think you will be able to say, 'I love Jesus.'"

The following Sunday the little girl came up to him again. With happy eyes and radiant face she exclaimed, "Oh, Mr. Pearse, I do love Jesus, I do love Jesus. Last Sunday as I went home I kept saying to myself, 'Jesus loves me. Jesus loves me. Jesus loves me.' And I began to think abut His love and I began to think how He died upon the cross in my place, and I found my cold heart growing warm, and the first I knew it was full of love to Jesus."

That is the only way anyone will ever learn to love the Lord Jesus—by first of all believing what the Bible tells us about His love for us even when we are the vilest of sinners, and how He died in our place; and how "He was wounded for our transgressions; he was bruised for our iniquities," and how "the chastisement of our peace was upon him"; and how "by his stripes we are healed." We begin by *believing on* Him, we begin by believing in His great love to us, and we wind up by loving Him and showing our love to Him by daily studying His Word to find out His will, and doing it every time we find it. Then we are on praying ground.

Some years ago a great Scotch teacher delivered an address at Northfield on the subject of whether it was better to have faith in Jesus Christ without love, or to have love for Jesus Christ without faith, and he came to the conclusion that it was better to have love without faith, than it was to have faith without love. But the whole address, though a great address in many ways, was built upon a misapprehension and a false assumption. He had assumed that we could have love without faith, but we cannot. Love to Christ is the outcome of faith in Christ, and faith in Christ is the root out of which love to Christ grows. To discuss whether it is better to have faith without love, or love without faith is like discussing whether it would be better to have an apple orchard whose trees had good roots but bore no apples; or to have an orchard whose trees had no roots but bore good apples. Of course an orchard where the trees had no roots would bear no apples at all. And a life that is not rooted in faith in the love of Jesus Christ to us has no roots and cannot bear the fruit of love, and the obedience which comes out of love. So, then, *this promise* that we are considering *is made to those who have a living faith in Jesus Christ that manifests itself in an obedient love.*

II. *Praying in the Name of Jesus*

But how must those who are united to Jesus Christ by a living faith that reveals itself in an obedient love pray if they are to get the very thing that they ask? Let us read the verse again: "And whatsoever ye shall ask *in my name,* that will I do, that the Father may be glorified in the Son. If ye shall ask anything *in my name,* that will I do." *If we are to get from God what we ask, we must ask it in the name of the Lord Jesus.* Prayer in the name of Jesus Christ prevails with God. No other prayer does. There is no other approach to

God for any man or woman except through Jesus Christ, as the Lord Himself tells us in the sixth verse of this same chapter: "I am the way, the truth, and the life: *no man cometh unto the Father, but by me.*"

But just what does it mean to pray in the name of Jesus? I have heard many explanations of this. Some of them were so profound or mystical, or so mixed, or so obscure, that when I finished reading them or listening to them I knew less about it than when I started. I have heard two great Bible teachers, two of the most renowned Bible teachers in the world, say that to "Pray in the name of Jesus means to pray in the person of Jesus." Now I do not question that these two great Bible teachers had some definite thought in their own minds, but it certainly conveyed no clear and definite thought to my mind. The truth is, there is nothing mysterious about this matter. It is as simple as anything possibly can be, so simple that any intelligent child can understand it. I am always suspicious of profound explanations of the Scriptures, explanations that require a scholar or philosopher to understand them. The Bible is the plain man's book. The Lord Jesus Himself said in Matthew 11:25, "I thank thee. O Father, Lord of heaven and earth, that thou didst hide these things from the wise and understanding, and didst reveal them unto *babes.*" In at least ninety-nine cases in a hundred the meaning of Scripture that lies on the surface, the meaning that any simple-minded man, woman, or child who really wants to know the truth and to obey it would see in it, is what it really means.

I have great sympathy with the little child who, when she once heard a learned attempt to explain away the plain meaning of Scripture, exclaimed, "If God did not mean what He said, why didn't He say what He meant?" Well, God always does say just what He means, just what you and I would understand by it if our wills were really surrendered to God and we really desired to know exactly what God wished to tell us— and not to read our own opinions into the Bible. By this expression, "In my name," He means just exactly what the words would indicate to any earnest and intelligent seeker after the truth who was willing to take God's words at their exact face value.

When you come across a word or a phrase in the Bible and do not know what it means, the thing to do is not to run off to a dictionary, or a commentary, or to some book of theology, but to take your concordance and go through the Bible and look up every place where that word or phrase, or synonymous words or phrases, are used. Then you will know just what the word or phrase means. The meaning of words and phrases in the Bible is to be determined just as it is in all other books, by usage. Now I have done this with this phrase, "In my name" and with synonymous phrases, "In his name" or "In the name of Jesus Christ." I have looked up every passage in the Bible where they are found, and I have discovered what I suspected at the outset, that these phrases mean exactly the same in the Bible that they do in ordinary everyday speech. What does it mean in ordinary everyday speech to ask something in some other person's name? It means simply this, that you ask the thing that you ask from the person of whom you ask it, on the ground of some claim that the person in whose name you ask it has upon the one from whom you ask it.

Let me illustrate. Suppose I should go down to the First National Bank of your city and should write out a check "Pay to the order of R. A. Torrey the sum of five dollars," and then should sign my own name at the bottom of the check and then go to the paying teller's window and put that check in. What would I be doing? I would be praying that bank to give me five dollars. And in whose name would I be asking it? In my own name. And what would happen? The paying teller would take the check and look at it, and then look at me, and then he would say "Dr. Torrey, have you any money in this bank?"

"No."

Then what would he say? Something like this. "We would like to accommodate you, but that is not good business. You have no claim whatever upon this bank and we cannot honor your check even though it is for only five dollars." But suppose, instead of that, some man in your city who had a hundred thousand dollars in that bank should call me in and say, "Dr. Torrey, I am greatly interested in the work of the Bible Institute, and I have wanted to give some money to it and I am going to hand it to you." And then he draws a check "Pay to the order of R. A. Torrey the sum of five thousand dollars," and then he signs his name at the bottom of the check. I go to the bank again, and in presenting that check what would I be doing? I would be asking that bank to give me five thousand dollars. And in whose name would I be asking it? Not in my own name, but in the name of the man whose name is signed to the bottom of the check, and who has claims of a hundred thousand dollars on that bank.

What would happen? The teller would look at the check, and then he would not ask me whether I had any money in that bank, and he would not care whether I had a penny in that bank or in any bank. If the check were properly drawn, and properly endorsed, he would count me out five thousand dollars; for I would be asking it in the other man's name, asking it on the ground of his claims on that bank.

Now that is exactly what praying in the name of Jesus Christ means. It means that we go to the bank of Heaven, on which neither you nor I nor any other man on earth has any claim of his own, but upon which Jesus Christ has infinite claims. In Jesus' name, which He has given us a right to put on our checks, if we are united to Him by a living faith that reveals itself in an obedient love, we may ask whatever we need in His name. Or, to put it another way, to pray in the name of Jesus Christ is to recognize that we have no claims on God whatever, that God owes us nothing whatever, that we deserve nothing of God; but, believing what God Himself tells us about Jesus Christ's claims upon Him, we ask God for things on the ground of Jesus Christ's claims upon God. And when we draw near to God in that way we can get "whatsoever we ask," no matter how great it may be.

Praying in the name of Christ means more than merely attaching that phrase, "In Jesus' name," or "For Jesus' sake" to your prayers. Many a man asks for things and puts that phrase, "In Jesus' name," or "For Jesus' sake" in his prayer, while all the time he is really approaching God on the ground of some claim that he fancies he has on God. In reality, though he uses the phrase, he is not praying in the name of Jesus Christ but praying in his own name. And a man might not put that phrase in his prayer at all, and yet all the time draw near to God realizing that he has no claims on God, but believing that Jesus Christ has claims on God and be approaching God on the ground of Jesus Christ's claims. Here is where many a person fails in getting an answer to prayer. Such people may ask things of God on the ground of some claim they fancy they themselves have on God. They fancy because they are such good Christians, so consistent in their lives, and so active in their service, that God is under obligation to grant their prayers.

In Melbourne, Australia, as I went on the platform one day at the business men's meeting, a note was put in my hands. This note read:

DEAR DR. TORREY:
I am in great perplexity. I have been praying for a long time for something that I am confident is according to God's will, but I do not get it. I have been a member of the Presbyterian Church for thirty years, and have tried to be a consistent one all the time. I have been Superintendent in the Sunday school for twenty-five years, and an elder in the church for twenty years; and yet God does not answer my prayer and I cannot understand it. Can you explain it to me?

I took the note with me on to the platform and read it and said, "It is perfectly easy to explain. This man thinks that because he has been a consistent church member for thirty years, a faithful Sunday school superintendent for twenty-five years, and an elder in the church for twenty years, that God is under obligation to answer his prayer. He is really praying in his own name, and God will not hear our prayers when we approach Him in that way. We must, if we would have God answer our prayers, give up any thought that we have any claims upon God. Not one of us deserves anything from God. If we got what we deserved, every last one of us would spend eternity in hell. But Jesus Christ has great claims on God, and we should go to God in our prayers not on the ground of any goodness in ourselves, but on the ground of Jesus Christ's claims.

106

And this man is going on the ground of the claims that he supposes that he has, because he has been a faithful church member for thirty years, a Sunday school superintendent for twenty-five years, and an elder in the church twenty years. He is praying in his own name. At the close of the meeting a gentleman stepped up to me and said, "I wrote that note. You have hit the nail square on the head. I did think that because I had been a consistent church member for thirty years, a Sunday school superintendent for twenty-five years, and an elder in the church for twenty years, that God was under obligation to answer my prayers. I see my mistake."

Multitudes are making the same mistake. They fancy that because they are faithful church members, and active in Christian service, that God is under obligation to answer their prayers, that they have some claim on God. Not one of us has any claim on God. We are miserable sinners. But Jesus Christ has claims on God and He has given us the right to draw near to God in His name, that is, on the ground of His claims on God.

To pray, then, in the name of Jesus Christ, means simply this: That we recognize that we have no claims whatever on God. That we have no merit whatsoever in His sight, and furthermore, that Jesus Christ has immeasurable claims on God, and has given us the right to draw near to God not on the ground of our claims, but on the ground of His claims. And when we thus draw near to God in prayer, God will give us what we ask.

What a precious privilege it is to pray in the name of Jesus Christ! How rich we are if we only realize that Jesus Christ has given us the privilege of drawing near to the Heavenly Father in His name, on the ground of His claims on God. When I was a boy my father had put the conduct of much of the expenditures of the home and other things in the hands of my brother next older than myself, my oldest brother being away from home. The bank account was in the name of this brother next older than myself. But he, too, was called away from home, and he turned over the matter of paying bills and conduct of the business to me. He gave me a check book full of checks made out in blank with his name signed to them and said, "Whenever you want any money just fill out this check for the amount that you want, and go and present it at the bank." How rich I felt with that bank book full of checks made out in blank. I could fill one out at any time and go to the bank and get what I asked. But what is that to what the Lord Jesus Christ has done for us? He has put all His bank account at our disposal. He has given us the right to draw near to the Father in His name, and ask anything of God on the ground not of our claims upon God, but on the ground of His claims upon God.

Even before Mr. Moody gave up business he was active in Christian work, and often went out from Chicago to some of the country towns and held short series of meetings. At one time he was holding a series of meetings in a town in Illinois some distance from Chicago. The wife of the judge of that district came to him and said, "Mr. Moody, won't you go and talk to my husband?"

Mr. Moody replied, "I cannot talk to your husband. Your husband is an educated man; I am nothing but an ignorant shoe clerk from Chicago."

But the judge's wife was very insistent that he should go and talk with him, and finally Mr. Moody consented to go—and he went. When he entered the outer office of the judge the law clerks tittered audibly as they thought of how quickly the clever judge would dispose of this ignorant young worker from Chicago. Mr. Moody went into the judge's inner office and said to him, "Judge, I cannot talk with you. You are an educated man, and I am nothing but an uneducated boot clerk from Chicago. But I want to ask you one thing. When you are converted will you let me know?"

The judge answered with a contemptuous laugh, "Yes, young man, when I am converted I will let you know. Yes, when I am converted I will let you know. Good morning."

As Mr. Moody passed out of the inner office to the outer office, the judge raised his voice higher so that the clerks in the outer office might hear, "Yes, young man, when I am converted I will let you know," and the law clerks tittered louder than before.

But the judge was converted within a year. Mr. Moody went back to the town and called on the judge.

He said, "Judge, do you mind telling me how you were converted?"

"No, Mr. Moody," he replied, "I will be very glad to tell you. Sometime after you were here, one prayer-meeting night my wife went to prayer-meeting as she always did, and I stayed home as I always did and read the evening paper. After a while as I sat there reading I began to feel very miserable. I began to feel that I was a great sinner. Before my wife got home I was so miserable that I did not dare face my wife and I retired before she reached the house. She came up to my room and asked, 'Are you ill?' I replied, 'No, I wasn't feeling well and thought I would go to bed. Good night.' I was miserable all night, and when morning came I felt so bad that I did not dare face my wife at the breakfast table, and I simply looked into the breakfast room and said, 'Wife, I am not feeling well. I'll not eat any breakfast this morning. Good-by, I am going down to the office.' When I got to the office I felt so miserable that I told my clerks that they could take a holiday, and when they had left I locked the outer door and then I went into my inner office and locked that door, and sat down. I felt more and more miserable as I thought of my sins, until at last I knelt down and said, 'Oh, God, forgive my sins.' There was no answer. And I cried more earnestly, 'Oh, God, forgive my sins.' There was still no answer. I would not say, 'Oh, God, for Jesus Christ's sake forgive my sins,' for I was a Unitarian and did not believe in the atonement. Again I cried, 'Oh, God, forgive my sins.' But there was no answer. At last I was so perfectly miserable at the thought of my sins that I cried, 'Oh, God, for Jesus Christ's sake forgive my sins.' And I found instant peace."

There is no use in our trying to approach God in any other way than in the name of Jesus Christ, and on the ground of His claims upon God, and on the ground of His atoning death whereby He took our sins upon Himself and made it possible for us to approach God on the ground of His claims upon God.

While we have no claims upon God because of any goodness or service of our own, Jesus Christ, as we have said, has infinite claims upon God and has given us the right to approach God in His name, and we ought to go boldly to God and ask great things of God. Oftentimes when we pray and ask something that seems to be pretty big, the devil will come and say to us, "You ought not to pray for anything so great as that, you are such a poor Christian that is more than you deserve." Yes, it is more than we deserve, but it is not as much as Jesus Christ deserves. Time and again Satan has said to me when I have dared to ask something of God that seemed very large, "Oh, don't dare to ask so great a thing as that. You are not worthy of anything so great as that," and I have replied, "I know that I am not worthy of anything so great as that. I am not worthy of anything at all, but Jesus Christ is worthy of that and I am asking not on the ground of my claims upon God, but on the ground of His." And sometimes as I think of how precious the name of Jesus Christ is to God, how He delights to honor the name of His Son, I grow very bold and ask God for great things.

Do you realize that we honor the name of Christ by asking great things in that name? Do you realize that we dishonor that name by not daring to ask great things in that name? Oh, have faith in the power of Jesus' name and dare to ask great things in His name.

During the Civil War there was a father and mother in Columbus, Ohio, who had an only son, the joy of their hearts. Soon after the outbreak of the war he came home one day and said to his father and mother, "I have enlisted in the army." Of course, they felt badly to have their son leave home, but they loved their country and were willing to make the sacrifice of giving their son to go to the war and fight for his country. After he had gone to the front he wrote home regularly, telling his father and mother about his experiences in camp and elsewhere. His letters were full of brightness and good cheer, and brought joy to the father's and mother's lonely hearts. But one day at the regular time no letter came.

Days passed, and no letter. Weeks passed, and they wondered what might have happened to their boy. One day a letter came from the United States Government and in it they were told that there had been a great battle, that many had been killed, and that their son was among those who had been killed in battle. The light went out of that home. Days and weeks, months and years passed by. The war came to an end. One morning as they were sitting at the breakfast table the maid came in and said, "There is a poor, ragged fellow out at the door and he wants to speak to you. But I knew you did not wish to speak to a man like him, and he handed me this note and asked me to put it in your hand." And she put in the hands of the father a soiled and crumpled piece of paper. The father opened it, and when he glanced at it his eyes fell upon the writing, then he started, for he recognized the writing of his son. The note said:

DEAR FATHER AND MOTHER:
I have been shot and have only a short time to live, and I am writing you this last farewell note. As I write there is kneeling beside me my most intimate friend in the company, and when the war is over he will bring you this note, and when he does be kind to him for Charlie's sake.
YOUR SON CHARLES

There was nothing in that house that was too good for that poor tramp, "For Charlie's sake," and there is nothing in heaven or on earth too good, or too great, for you and me in Jesus' name. Oh, be bold and ask great things of God *in Jesus' name.*

7

"THE PRAYER OF FAITH"

"And this is the confidence that we have in him, that, if we ask anything according to his will, he heareth us; And if we know that he heareth us, whatsoever we ask, we know that we have the petitions that we have asked of him."—I JOHN 5:14, 15, cf. R.V.

This is one of the most remarkable statements to be found in the whole Bible. It deals with God answering prayer, and our knowing that God has heard our prayer and granted the thing we have asked of Him. Look at it again:

"And this is *the confidence* that we have in him, that *if we ask anything according to his will* he heareth us: and if we know that he heareth us, whatsoever we ask, *we know that we have the petitions that we have asked of him.*" (See R. V.)

Please note carefully exactly what God tells us in this passage. We are told that there is a way in which certain people can pray so as not only to get the very thing that they ask, but *so as to know before* they actually get it, that God has heard their prayer and that therefore the thing which they have asked of Him He has granted to them. Certainly that is an astonishing statement: it gives to us the plain and positive assurance that there are some people who can pray in a certain way, and that if those people pray in that way they will not only get whatsoever they ask, but furthermore they may *know before they get it* that God has heard their prayer and *granted the thing they have asked*. It is

112

certainly a great joy when one prays to be able to know that the prayer we have offered has been heard and the thing which we have asked has been granted, and to be just as sure that it is ours as we shall afterwards be when we actually have it in our hand.

I. *To Whom the Promise Is Made*

Please note, first of all, *just who it is to whom God makes this promise.* As I have said so often before, when you try to understand and apply the promises of God which you find in the Bible, you must always be very careful to note just exactly who the people are to whom the promise is made. Just who the persons are to whom this promise is made we are told in the immediate context, in the verse that immediately precedes, "These things have I written unto you, that ye may know that ye have eternal life, *even unto you that believe on the name of the Son of God."* Then immediately follows the promise that we are studying, so it is clear that the promise is made to those who "believe on the name of the Son of God," to them and to no one else, and anyone who does not believe on the name of the Son of God has no right whatever to take this promise to himself, or to think that if he does take the promise to himself and it is not fulfilled that God's Word has failed. The fault is with himself, and not with God's Word. He has taken to himself a promise that was made to someone else. Just what it means to believe on the Son of God we are told in the gospel that was written by the same one who wrote this epistle. In John 1:12 we are told: "But as many as *received him* [that is, received Jesus Christ], to them gave he the right to become children of God, even to them that *believe on his name."*

So John himself interprets "believing on the name of the Son of God" to mean receiving the Son of God, that is, receiving Him to be to ourselves what He offers Himself to be to all who put their trust in Him, our personal Savior who bore our sins in His own body on the cross, and our Lord and Master to whom we surrender the absolute control of our thoughts, our will, and our conduct. So, then, this promise is made to

113

those who have received Jesus Christ as their personal Savior and trusted God to forgive them because Jesus Christ died on the cross in their place, and who have also received Him as their Lord and Master to whom they have surrendered the absolute control of their thoughts, their will, and their conduct, those who have made an absolute surrender to Jesus Christ, the Son of God. It is made to them, and to no one else, and no one else has the least right to claim it.

Just here is where many go astray; they do not really "believe on the name of the Son of God," they have not really "received him," yet they appropriate to themselves this promise that was never made to them.

II. *How We Must Pray in Order to Know That God Has Heard Our Prayers and Granted the Thing That We Have Asked*

Now we come to the question, *How must "those who believe on the name of the Son of God" pray in order to know that God has heard their prayer, and granted the thing that they asked?* Read I John 5:14 again. "And this is the confidence that we have in him, that, if we ask anything *according to his will,* he heareth us." To know that God has heard our prayer and granted us the thing we asked, we must *pray according to His will.* When we who believe on the name of the Son of God pray for anything that we know to be according to His will, then we may know, for the all-sufficient reason that God says so in His Word, that God has heard the prayer and granted us the thing that we ask. We may know it not because we feel it, not because of any inward illumination of the Holy Spirit. We may know it for the very best of all reasons—because God says so in His Word, and "God cannot lie."

But is it possible for us to know what the will of God is, so that we can be sure while we are praying that we are asking something that is *"according to His will"*? We certainly can know the will of God with absolute certainty in many cases when we pray. *How can we know the will of God?*

1. In the first place, *We may know the will of God by the promises in His Word.* The Bible was given us

114

for the specific purpose of revealing to us the will of God, and when we find that anything is definitely promised in the Word of God we know that that is His will, for He has said so in so many words. And when we who believe on the name of the Son of God go to God and ask Him for anything that is definitely promised in His Word, we may know with absolute certainty that God has heard our prayer and that the thing which we have asked of God is granted. We do not have to feel it—*God says so, and that is enough.*

For example, God says in James 1:5 (R.V.), "If any of you lacketh wisdom, let him ask of God, who giveth to all liberally and upbraideth not; and it shall be given him." So when I go to God and ask for wisdom, if I am a believer on the name of the Son of God, I know with absolute certainty that God has heard my prayer and that wisdom will be granted.

Some years ago I was speaking on the subject of prayer at a Y.M.C.A. Bible Conference at Mahtomede, White Bear Lake, Minnesota. I had to hurry immediately from the amphitheatre to the train. As I passed out of the amphitheatre I saw another minister from Minneapolis. He was to immediately follow me on the program, and was greatly excited. He stopped me and said, "Mr. Torrey, I am going to tear to pieces everything that you have said to these young men this morning."

I replied, "If I have not spoken according to the Bible, I hope you will tear it to pieces. But if I have spoken according to the Book you better be careful how you try to tear it to pieces."

"But," he exclaimed, "you have produced upon these young men the impression that they can pray for things and get the very thing that they ask for."

I replied, "I do not know whether that is the impression that I have produced or not, but it certainly is the impression I intended to produce."

"But," he said, "that is not right; you must say if it be according to God's will."

I replied, "If you do not know that the thing which you have asked is according to God's will, then it is all right to say, If it be according to Thy will. But if you know God's will, what is the need of saying, If it be according to Thy will?"

"But," he said, "we cannot know God's will."

I answered, "What was the Bible given to us for if it was not to reveal God's will? Now," I said, "when you find a definite promise in the Bible and take that promise to God, don't you know that you have asked something according to His will? For example, we read in James 1:5, 'If any of you lacketh wisdom, let him ask of God, who giveth to all liberally and upbraideth not; and it shall be given him.' Now," I said, "when you ask for wisdom do you not know that God is going to give it?"

"But," he said, "I do not know what wisdom is."

I said, "If you did you would not need to ask it, but whatever it may be, do you not know that God is going to give it?" He made no reply. I never heard that he tried to tear what I said to pieces, but I know that later he himself spoke boldly on the subject of confidently asking God for the things that we need of Him, and that are according to His will.

No, when you have a definite promise in God's Word you do not need to put any "ifs" before it. All the promises of God are yea and amen in Christ Jesus (II Cor. 1:20). They are absolutely sure, and if you plead any plain promise in God's Word you need not put any "ifs" in your petition. You may know that you are asking something that is according to God's will, and it is your privilege to know that God has heard you; and it is your privilege to know that you have the thing you have asked; it is your privilege to get up from prayer with the same absolute certainty that that thing is yours that you will afterward have when you actually see it in your hand.

Suppose some cold winter morning when I lived in Chicago I had gone down on South Clark street. It was then teeming with poor men. Suppose some shivering tramp should have come up to me and said, "Mr. Torrey, it is very cold and I need an overcoat. Will you give me an overcoat?" And then I had replied, "If you will come over to my house this afternoon at 39 East Pearson Street, at two o'clock, I'll give you an overcoat." Promptly at two o'clock the tramp makes his appearance. I meet him at the door and bring him into the house. Then he says to me, "Mr. Torrey, you said to me this morning on South Clark Street that if I would come to your house at two o'clock this afternoon you would give me an overcoat. Now, *if you will,* please give me that overcoat." What would I say? I'd say, "Man, what did you say?" "I said, *if you will,* please give me that overcoat." "But why do you put any 'if' in? Did I not say I would?" "Yes." "Do you doubt my word?" "No." "Then why do you put in an 'if'?"

Why should we put any "ifs" in when we take to God any promise of His own? Does God ever lie? There are many cases in which we do not know the will of God, and in such cases it is all right to put in "if it be Thy will." And even in cases where we do know His will, our prayers should always be in submission to His will, for the dearest of anything to the true child of God is God's will, but there is no need to put any "ifs" in when He has revealed His will. To put in an "if" in such a case as that is to doubt God, to doubt His Word, and really is to "make God a liar."

This passage of Scripture is one of the most abused passages in the Bible. God put it into His Word to give us "confidence" when we pray. It is constantly misused to make us uncertain when we pray. Often when some young and enthusiastic believer is asking for something with great confidence, some cautious brother will go to him after the meeting is over and say to him, "Now, my young brother, you must not be so confident as that in your prayers. It may not be God's will, and we ought to be submissive to the will of God, and you should say, 'If it be Thy will.' " And so some men always have an element of uncertainty in their prayers, and one would think that I John 5:14 read, "This is the *uncertainty* that we have in Him, that we can never know God's will, and therefore can never be sure that our prayer is heard." But that is not the way the verse reads. It reads, "This is the *confidence* (not uncertainty, but absolute confidence) that we have in him, that, if we ask anything according to his will, *he heareth us:* And if we know that he hear us, whatsoever we ask, *we know that we have* the petitions that we have asked of him." Oh, how subtle the devil is to take a passage of

Scripture that God has put into His Word to fill us with confidence when we pray, and use it to make us uncertain when we pray.

2. *But can we know the will of God when we pray, even when there is no definite promise in regard to the matter about which we are praying?* Yes, in many cases we can. How? Romans 8:26, 27 R. V. answers the question: "And in like manner *the Spirit* also *helpeth our infirmity:* for *we know not* how to pray as we ought; *but the Spirit* himself maketh intercession for us with groanings which cannot be uttered; and he that searcheth the hearts knoweth what is the mind of the Spirit, because *he maketh intercession for the saints according to the will of God."* It is the work of the Holy Spirit when we pray to make known to us what is the will of God in the matter about which we are praying, and to show us (if the thing *is* according to His will) that it is according to His Will. We need many things which are not definitely promised in the Word, and it doesn't follow at all that because they are not definitely promised in the Word that they are not "according to the will of God." It is the will of God to give us many things which He has not definitely promised in His Word, and it is the method of God, when we pray, to give us, by the direct illumination of the Holy Spirit, to know His will even in regard to things about which He has given us no definite promise.

For example, while I was pastor of the Moody Church in Chicago, the little daughter of a man and woman who were both members of our church was taken very ill. She first had the measles, and the measles were followed by meningitis. She sank very low, and the doctor said to her mother, "I can do no more for your child. She cannot live." The mother immediately hurried down to my house to get me to come up to their house and pray for her child. But I was out of town holding meetings in Pittsburgh. So she sent for the assistant pastor, Rev. W. S. Jacoby, and he went up to the house with one of my colleagues, and prayed for the child. That night when I got home from Pittsburgh he came around to my house to tell me about it, and he said, "Mr. Torrey, if I ever had an answer to my prayers in my life, it was today when I

118

was praying for the Duff child." He was confident that God had heard his prayer and that the child would be healed. And the child was healed right away. This was Saturday.

The next morning the doctor called again at the home and there was such a remarkable change in the child that he said to Mrs. Duff, "What have you done for your child?" She told him just what she had done.

Then he said, "Well, I will give her some more medicine."

"No," she said, "you will not. You said you could do no more for her, that she must die and we went to God in prayer and God has healed her. You are not going to take the honor to yourself by giving her some more medicine." Indeed, the girl was not only improved that morning, she was completely well.

Now, neither Mr. Jacoby nor I could pray for every sick child in that way, for it is not the will of God to heal every sick child, nor every sick adult. It is God's general will in regard to His children that they be well in body, but there are cases when God for wise purposes of His own does not see fit to heal the sick; there are cases when He does see fit to heal the sick, and in those cases if we are living near to God and listening for the voice of His Spirit, and are entirely surrendered to the Spirit in our praying, the Spirit of God will make clear to us the will of God, and we will *know* that our prayer is heard; and we will know that the thing is ours long before we actually get it.

Here is another illustration along an entirely different line. The healing of the body is only one of the lines along which God answers prayer, and not by any means the most important. In my first pastorate we had a union meeting of all the churches of the town. In the course of the meetings we had a day of fasting and prayer. During the morning meeting as we were praying God led me to pray that one of the most unlikely men in the town might be saved that night. He had led a wild life; few of his family were Christians; but as we knelt in prayer that morning God put a great burden on my heart for that man's salvation, and I prayed that he might come to the meeting and be saved that night. And as I prayed God gave me a great confidence that he would come and be saved that night. And come he did, and he was saved. There was not a man in that whole town who was more unlikely to be saved than he. That was more than forty years ago, but when I was down in Chattanooga, Tennessee, a few years ago I met another man whose mother was saved about the same time, and he told me that this man was then living in Tennessee and was still living a Christian life. Now I cannot pray for the salvation of every unsaved person in that way, but God by His Spirit revealed to me His will regarding that man, and in many a case He has thus revealed His Will.

Take an illustration along still another line. One day in Northfield, Mass., I received word from Chicago from Mr. Fitt, Mr. Moody's son-in-law, that we needed $5,000.00 at once for the work in Chicago, and asking me to pray for it. Another member of the faculty of the Bible Institute was in Northfield at that time, and that night we went out into a summer-house on my place and knelt down and prayed God to send that money. And God gave my friend great confidence that He had heard the prayer, and he said to me, "God has heard the prayer and the five thousand dollars will come." Mr. Fitt and Mr. Gaylord also prayed in Chicago, and God gave Mr. Gaylord a great confidence that the money would come. We knew it was ours, we knew that God had heard the prayer and that we had received the five thousand dollars. And a telegram came the next day (I think it was)from Indianapolis, saying $5,000.00 had been deposited in a bank in Indianapolis to our account and was waiting our order. Though we had prayed and expected, Mr. Fitt could hardly believe it when he heard it, and sent down to our bank in Chicago and they made inquiry from the bank in Indianapolis if it were true. They found out that it was. As far as I know, the man who put that money in the bank in Indianapolis at our call had never given a penny to the Bible Institute before. I did not know there was such a man in the world, and as far as I know he has never given a penny to the Bible Institute since. Now I cannot go to God every time I want money and think I need it and ask God for it with that same confidence, but there are times when I can. There have

120

been many such times in my life, and God has never failed, and He never will. Banks sometimes fail; God never fails.

To sum it all up, when God makes His will known, either by a specific promise of His Word or by His Holy Spirit while we are praying, that the thing that we ask for is "according to His will," it is our privilege to know—if we really believe on the name of the Son of God—that that thing we have asked is granted, and that it is ours; just as truly ours as it will be when afterwards we actually have it in our hand.

III. *Praying in Faith*

The passage we have been studying is closely related to another passage in the gospel of Mark, that contains a promise of our Lord Himself in regard to God anwering prayer. It is a familiar passage; you will find it in Mark 11:24, "Therefore I say unto you, What things soever *ye* desire, when ye pray, *believe that ye receive them and ye shall have them.*" I will not stop to call your attention to whom this promise is made, further than to say that it is made as are all the other promises of God to those who believe on Jesus Christ, those who are united to Jesus Christ by a living faith that manifests itself in an obedient love. This is evident from the context, as you can find out for yourself if you will read the promise in its context.

And *how must we pray in order to get the thing that we ask? We must pray in faith,* that is, we must pray with a confident expectation of getting the very thing that we ask. There are those who say that any prayer that is in submission to the will of God, and in faith in Him and dependence on God, is a prayer of faith. But it is not *"the* prayer of faith" in the Bible sense of "the prayer of faith." *"The prayer of faith"* in the Bible sense of "the prayer of faith," is *the prayer that has no doubt whatever that God has heard the prayer and granted the specific thing "which we have asked of Him."* This is evident from James 1:5-7 R. V.: "But if any of you lacketh wisdom, let him ask of God, who giveth to all liberally and upbraideth not; and it shall be given him. But let him ask in faith *nothing doubt-*

ing: for *he that doubteth* is like the surge of the sea driven by the wind and tossed. For *let not that man think that he shall receive anything of the Lord."* No matter how positive the promises of God may be, we will never receive them in our own experience till we absolutely believe them, and the prayer that gets what it asks is "the prayer of faith," that is, the prayer that has no doubt whatever of getting the very thing that is asked.

This comes out more clearly in the Revised Version of Mark 11:24 than in the Authorized. Let me read you from the English Revision, which is more accurate in this case than the American Revision: "Therefore I say unto you, all things whatsoever ye pray and ask for, *believe that ye have received them,* and ye shall have them." When we pray to God, and pray according to His will as known by the promises of His Word, or as known by the Holy Spirit revealing His will to us, we should confidently believe that the very thing we have asked is granted us. We should "believe that" we *"have* received," and what we thus believe we have received we shall afterwards have in actual personal experience.

Take, for example, the matter of praying for "the baptism with the Holy Spirit." When anyone prays for the Holy Spirit, anyone who is united to Jesus Christ by a living faith that reveals itself in an obedient love, anyone who has received Jesus Christ as their Savior and is trusting God to forgive them on the sole ground that Jesus Christ died in their place, and who has received Jesus Christ as their Lord and Master, and surrendered all their thoughts and purposes and conduct to His control, they may know that they have prayed for something according to His will, for Jesus Christ definitely says in Luke 11:13, "If ye then, being evil, know how to give good gifts unto your children; how *much more shall your heavenly Father give the Holy Spirit to them that ask him?"* And as he knows that he has asked something which is according to God's will as He has clearly revealed it in His Word, it is his privilege to say, "I have what I asked. I have the Holy Spirit."

It is not a question at all of whether he feels that he has received the Holy Spirit or not; it is not a question

122

of some remarkable experience: it is simply a question of taking God at His Word and that the one who prays believes that he has received, *just because God says so.* What he has taken by naked faith on the Word of God, simply believing he has received, because God says so, he will afterwards have in actual experimental possession. There is no need that he go to any "tarrying meeting," no need that he work himself up into a frenzy of emotionalism, no need that he fall into a trance, or fall into unconsciousness, an experience utterly foreign to anything described in the New Testament. He has a far better ground for his assurance that he has received what he asked than any feeling or any ecstasy; he has the immutable Word of God, "God who cannot lie."

Praying in faith, that is, praying with an unquestioning belief that you will receive just exactly what you ask; yes, believing as you pray that God has heard your prayer and that you have received the thing that you ask, is one of the most important factors in obtaining what we ask when we pray. As James puts it in James 1:6, 7, "Let him ask in faith, *nothing doubting:* for he that doubteth is like the surge of the sea driven by the wind and tossed. For *let not that man think that he shall receive anything of the Lord.*" That is, let not the man who has any doubts that God has heard his prayer, think that he shall receive anything of the Lord.

So the tremendously important question arises, How can we pray the prayer of faith? How can we pray with a confident, unquestioning certainty in our minds, that God has heard our prayer and granted the thing that we ask? This has been partly answered in what we have already said, but in order that it may be perfectly clear, let us repeat the substance of it again.

1. *To pray the prayer of faith we must,* first of all, *study the Word of God, especially the promises of God, and find out what the will of God is and build our prayers on the written promises of God.* Intelligent faith, and that is the only kind of faith that counts with God, must have a warrant. We cannot believe by just trying to make ourselves believe. Such belief as that is not faith but credulity; it is "make believe."

The great warrant for intelligent faith is God's Word.

123

As Paul puts it in Romans 10:17, "Faith cometh by hearing, and hearing by the word of God." The faith that is built upon the sure Word of God is an intelligent faith, it has something to rest upon. So if we would pray the prayer of faith we must study much the Word of God, and find out what God has definitely promised, and then with God's promise in mind approach God and ask Him for that thing which He has promised.

Here is the point at which many go astray. Here is the point at which I went astray in my early prayer life. Not long after my conversion I got hold of this promise of our Lord Jesus in Mark 11:24, "Therefore I say unto you, What things soever ye desire, when ye pray, *believe that ye receive them,* and ye shall have them." I said to myself, "All that I need to do if I want anything is to ask God for it and then make myself believe that I am going to get it, and I'll have it." So whenever I wanted anything I asked God for it and tried to make myself believe I was going to get it, but I didn't get it, for it was only "make-believe," and I did not really believe at all. But I later learned that "faith cometh by hearing, and hearing by the Word of God," and that if I wished to pray "the prayer of faith" I must have some warrant for my faith, some ground upon which to rest my faith, and that the surest of all grounds for faith was the Word of God. So when I desired anything of God I would search the Scriptures to find if there was some promise that covered that case, and then go to God and plead His own promise; and thus resting upon that promise I would believe that God had heard, and He had, and I got what I asked.

One of the mightiest men of prayer of the last generation was George Mueller of Bristol, England, who in the last sixty years of his life (he lived to be ninety-two or ninety-three) obtained the English equivalent of $7,200,000.00 by prayer. But George Mueller never prayed for a thing just because he wanted it, or even just because he felt it was greatly needed for God's work. When it was laid upon George Mueller's heart to pray for anything, he would search the Scriptures to find if there was some promise that covered the case. Sometimes he would search the Scriptures for days before he presented his petition to God. And then when he found the promise, with his open Bible before him and his finger upon that promise, he would plead that promise and so he received what he asked. He always prayed with an open Bible before him.

2. But this is not all that is to be said about how to pray the prayer of faith. It is possible for us to have faith in many an instance when there is no definite promise covering the case, and to pray with the absolute assurance that God has heard our prayer, to believe with a faith that has not a shadow of a doubt in it, that we have received what we have asked. The way that comes to pass we are plainly told in the passage to which I have already referred in the earlier part of this chapter, Romans 8:26, 27 R.V. "In like manner the Spirit also helpeth our infirmity: for we know not how to pray as we ought; but the Spirit himself maketh intercession for us with groanings which cannot be uttered, and he that searcheth the hearts knoweth what is the mind of the Spirit, because *he* maketh intercession for the saints *according to the will of God.*" That is to say, *the Holy Spirit,* as we have already said, *often makes clear to us as we pray what it is the will of God to do, so that listening to His voice we can pray with absolute confidence, with a confidence that has not a shadow of doubt, that God has heard our prayer and granted the thing that we asked.*

My first experience, at least the first that I recall, of this wonderful privilege of knowing the will of God, and praying with confident faith even when one had no definite promise in the written Word that God would hear the prayer, came early in my ministry. There was a young dentist in my congregation whose father was a member of our church. This dentist was taken very ill with typhoid fever; he went down to the very gates of death. I went to see him and found him unconscious. The doctor and his father were by the bedside, and the doctor said to me, "He cannot live. The crisis is past and it has turned the wrong way. There is no possibility of his recovery." I knelt down to pray, and as I prayed a great confidence came into my heart, an absolutely unshakable confidence that God had heard my prayer and that that man was to be raised up. As I got up

125

from my knees I said to the father and the doctor, "Ebbie will get well. He will not die at this time."

The doctor smiled and said, "That is all right, Mr. Torrey, from your standpoint, but he cannot live. He will die."

I replied, "Doctor, that is all right from your standpoint, but he cannot die; he will live." I went to my home. Not long after word was brought to me that the young man was dying. They told me what he was doing, and said that no one ever did that except just when they were dying. I calmly replied, "He is not dying. He will not die. He will get well." I knew he would: he did. The last I knew he was living yet, and his healing took place between forty and forty-five years ago.

But I cannot pray for every sick man in that way, not even though he is an earnest Christian, which this man was not at that time. Sometimes it is God's will to heal, usually it is God's will to heal, if the conditions are met; but it is not always God's will to heal. "The *prayer of faith* shall save the sick," God tells us in James 5:15; but it is not always possible to pray "the prayer of faith," only when God makes it possible by the leading of His Holy Spirit.

But "the prayer of faith" will not only heal the sick, it will bring many other blessings, blessings of far more importance than physical healing. It will bring salvation to the lost; it will bring power into our service; it will bring money into the treasury of the Lord; it will bring great revivals of religion. In my first pastorate one of the first persons to accept Christ was a woman who had been a backslider for many years. But she not only came back to the Lord, she came back in a very thorough way. Not long after her conversion God gave to her a great spirit of prayer for a revival in our church and community. When I had been there about a year she was called to go out to California with a sick friend, but before going she came into the prayer-meeting on her last prayer-meeting night there, and said, "God has heard my prayer for a revival. You are going to have a great revival here in the church." And we did have a revival not only in the church but in the whole community, a revival that transformed every church in the community, and brought many souls to

126

Christ. And the revival went on again the next year, and the next, and the next until I left that field. And it went on under the pastor who followed me, and the pastor who followed him.

Oh, yes, "the prayer of faith" is the great secret of getting what we need in our personal life; what we need in our service; what we need in our work; what we need in our church; what we need everywhere. There is no limit to what "the prayer of faith can do"; and if we would pray more and pray more intelligently, and pray 'the prayer of faith," there is no telling what we could do. But as we have said, to pray "the prayer of faith" we must first of all study our Bibles intensely that we may know the promises of God, what they are, how large they are, how definite they are, and just exactly what is promised. In addition to that we must live so near to God, be so fully surrendered to the will of God, have such a delight in God and so feel our utter dependence upon the Spirit of God, that the Holy Spirit Himself can guide us in our prayers and indicate clearly to us what the will of God is, and make us sure while we pray that we have asked for something that is according to God's will, and thus enable us to pray with the absolute confidence that God has heard our prayer, and that "we have received" the things that we asked of Him.

Here is where many of us fail in our prayer lives: we either do not know that it is our privilege to "pray in the Spirit," that is, to pray under the Spirit's guidance; or else we do not realize our utter dependence upon the Holy Spirit, and cast ourselves upon Him to lead us when we pray, and therefore we pray for the things which our own hearts prompt us to pray for, our own selfish desires; or else we are not in such an attitude toward God that the Spirit of God can make His voice heard in our hearts.

Oh, that we might all be made to realize the immeasurable blessings for ourselves, for our friends, and for the church and for the world, that lie within the reach of "the prayer of faith," and determine that we will pray the prayer of faith; and then get down to the study of the Word of God so that we could know God's will and what to pray for; and be in such a relationship toward

127

God, be fully surrendered to His will and delight in Himself, and in utter, constant dependence upon the Holy Spirit, looking to the Holy Spirit that as we pray it might not be so much we who pray as the Holy Spirit praying through us. Then we would soon see our spiritually dead cities and our spiritually dead churches, "blossom as the rose."

8

PRAYING THROUGH: AND PRAYING IN THE HOLY SPIRIT

"Men ought always to pray, and not to faint."—LUKE 18:1.

"Though he will not rise and give him, because he is his friend, yet because of his importunity he will rise and give him as many as he needeth. And I say unto you, Ask, and it shall be given you; seek, and ye shall find; knock, and it shall be opened unto you."—LUKE 11:8, 9.

"With all prayer and supplication praying at all seasons in the Spirit, and watching thereunto in all perseverance and supplication for all the saints."—EPH. 6:18.

I. *Praying Through*

There are two passages in the gospel of Luke which throw a flood of light upon the question, What sort of praying it is that prevails with God and obtains what it seeks from Him; and also upon the question, Why it is that many prayers of God's own children come short of obtaining that which we seek of God. The first of these two passages you will find in Luke 11:5-8; our Lord Himself is the speaker:

> And He said unto them, Which of you shall have a friend, and shall go unto him at midnight, and say unto him, Friend, lend me three loaves; For a friend of mine is come to me from a journey, and I have

129

nothing to set before him and he from within shall answer and say, Trouble me not: the door is now shut, and my children are with me in bed; I cannot rise and give thee? I say unto you, Though he will not rise and give him because he is his friend, yet *because of his importunity* he will arise and give him as many as he needeth. And I say unto you, Ask, and it shall be given you; seek, and ye shall find; knock, and it shall be opened unto you. For every one that asketh receiveth; and he that seeketh findeth; and to him that knocketh it shall be opened.

The central lesson in this parable of our Lord's is, that, *When we pray, if we do not obtain the thing the first time we ask for it, we should pray again; and if we do not obtain it the second time, we should pray a third time; and if we do not obtain it the hundredth time we pray, we should go on praying until we do get it.* We should do much thinking before we ask anything of God and be clear that the thing that we ask is according to His will; we should not rush heedlessly into God's presence and ask for the first thing that comes into our minds without giving proper thought to the question of whether it is really a thing that we ought to have or not; but *when we have decided that we should pray for the thing, we should keep on praying until we get it.* The word translated "importunity" in the eighth verse is a deeply significant word. Its primary meaning is "shamelessness," that is, it sets forth the persistent determination in prayer to God that will not be put to shame by any apparent refusal on God's part to grant the thing that we ask. This is a very startling way that our Lord Jesus employs to set forth the necessity of "importunity" and persistence in prayer. It is as if the Lord Jesus would have us understand that God would have us draw nigh to Him with a resolute determination to obtain the things that we seek, a determination that will not be put to shame by any seeming refusal or delay on God's part.

Our Heavenly Father delights in the holy boldness on our part that will not take "no" for an answer. The reason why He delights in it is, because it is an expres-

130

sion of great faith, and nothing pleases God more than faith. We have an illustration of this holy boldness in the woman of Syro-Phoenicia in Matthew 15:21-28. She came to Jesus Christ for the healing of her daughter. She cried, "Have mercy on me, O Lord, thou Son of David; my daughter is grievously vexed with a demon." But our Lord seemed to pay no attention whatever to her; as Matthew puts it, "He answered her not a word. And his disciples came [to him] and besought him saying, Send her away for she crieth after us." In spite of His apparent deafness to her appeal she kept right on crying. Then He turned to her with an apparently more positive rebuff, saying, "I was not sent but unto the lost sheep of the house of Israel," and she was not of the House of Israel. Then she worshiped Him and kept on calling to Him, saying, "Lord, help me." And then came what almost appears like a cruel rebuff, when our Lord said, "It is not meet to take the children's bread and cast it to the dogs." (The word that He used for "dogs" was a peculiar word that meant a little pet dog, and was not at all as harsh as it seems, although it was an apparent refusal to hear her prayer. But, as we shall see, our Lord was simply putting to the test her faith that she might receive an even larger blessing.) Then she said, "Yea, Lord: for even the dogs eat of the crumbs which fall from their master's table." She would not take "no" for an answer. And then came one of the most wonderful words of commendation that ever fell from the lips of our Lord. This is the way Matthew put it: "Then Jesus answered and said unto her, O woman, great is thy faith: be it done unto thee even as thou wilt. And her daughter was healed from that hour." That sort of thing pleases God. He would have us have that faith in His loving kindness and in Himself that even when He seems not to hear will trust Him still to hear.

God does not always give us the things we ask the first time we ask them, but then we should not give up; no, we should keep on praying until we do receive. We should not only pray, but we should *pray through*.

It is deeply significant that this parable to persist in prayer comes almost immediately after the request on the part of the disciples of our Lord, in which they say,

"Lord, teach us to pray." Then follows Luke's version of the so-called "Lord's Prayer," really the disciples' prayer, and then comes this parable.

The same lesson is taught in a striking way in the second passage in Luke to which I have already referred, Luke 18:1-8: "And he spake a parable unto them to the end that *they ought always to pray, and not to faint;* saying, There was in a city a judge, who feared not God, and regarded not man: and there was a widow in that city; and she came oft unto him, saying, Avenge me of mine adversary. And *he would not for a while:* but afterward he said within himself, Though I fear not God, nor regard man; yet because this widow troubleth me, I will avenge her, lest she wear me out *by her continual coming.* And the Lord said, Hear what the unrighteous judge saith. And *shall not God* avenge His elect, that cry to Him day and night, and yet He is long-suffering over them? I say unto you, that He will avenge them speedily. Nevertheless, when the Son of man cometh, shall he find faith (literally, 'the faith') on the earth?" What the central lesson in this parable is, we find in the words with which our Lord Jesus opens the parable, which are really the text of the whole parable; these words are, "Men ought always to pray, *and not to faint,"* the clear meaning of which is, that when we begin to pray to ought to pray on and on until we get the thing that we desire of God. The exact force of the parable is, that if even an unrighteous judge will yield to persistent prayer and grant the thing that he did not wish to grant, how much more will a loving God yield to the persistent cries of His children and give the things that He longs to give all the time, but which it would not be wise to give, would not be for the person's own good to give, unless they were trained to that persevering faith that will not take "no" for an answer. So we see again that God does not always give us at the first asking what we desire of Him in prayer.

Why is it that God does not give to us the very first time we ask Him, the things that we ask of Him? The answer is plain: God would do more for us, and better for us, than to give us merely that thing. He would do us the far greater good of training us into *persistent*

132

faith. The things that we get by our other forms of effort than prayer to God, do not always become ours the first time we make an effort to get them; for our own good God compels us to be persistent in our effort, and just so God does not always give us what we ask in prayer the first time we pray. Just as He would train us to be strong men and women along the other lines of effort, so also He would train us to be and make us to be strong men and women of prayer by compelling us to pray hard for the best things. He compels us to *"pray through."*

Many people in these days tell us that we ought not to pray for the same thing a second time. Sometimes they tell us that the way to pray is to ask God for a thing and then "take it" by faith the first time we ask. That is often true: when we find a thing definitely promised in the Word we ought to rest upon the naked Word of God, and when we have prayed, know that we have asked something according to God's will and therefore that the prayer is heard and that we have received; and resting there ask no more but claim the thing as ours. But that is only one side of the truth. The other side of the truth is, that there are times when it is not made clear the first time, nor the second time, nor the third time, that the thing we ask is according to His will and that therefore the prayer is heard and the thing asked granted; and in such a case we ought to pray on and on and on. While doubtless there are times when we are able through faith in the Word, or through the clear leading of the Holy Spirit, to *claim* a thing the first time that we have asked it of God; nevertheless, beyond a question there are other times when we must pray again and again and again for the same thing before we get our answer. Those who claim that they have gotten beyond praying twice for the same thing have either gotten beyond our Master, our Lord and Savior Jesus Christ, or else they have not gotten up to Him; for we are told distinctly regarding Him in Matthew 26:44, "And he left them again, and went away, *and prayed a third time, saying again the same words."* The truth is they have not yet gotten up to the Master; not that they have gotten beyond Him.

There are those, and there are many of them, who,

when they pray for a thing once or twice and do not get it, stop praying; and they call it "submission to the will of God" to pray no longer when God does not grant their request at the first or second asking. They say, "Well, perhaps it is not God's will." They call that submission to the will of God. But as the rule this is not submission to the will of God: it is spiritual laziness and lack of determination in that most all-important of all human lines of effort, prayer. None of us ever think of calling it submission to the will of God, when we give up after one or two efforts to obtain things by other efforts than prayer. In those cases we call it lack of strength of character. When the strong man of action starts out to accomplish a thing, if he does not accomplish it the first, or the second, or the hundredth time, he keeps hammering away until he does accomplish it; and just so the strong man of prayer, when he starts to pray for a thing, keeps on praying until he prays it through and obtains what he seeks. How fond we are of calling bad things in our conduct by good names, calling our spiritual inertia and laziness and indifference "submission to the will of God." We should be careful about what we ask from God, but when we do begin to pray for a thing we should never give up praying for it until we get it, or until God definitely makes it very clear to us that it is not His will to give it.

I am glad that God does not always give us, the first time we ask, the things that we seek from Him. There is no more blessed training in prayer than that which comes through being compelled to ask again and again and again, even through a long period of years, before one obtains that which he seeks from God. Then when it does come what a sense we have that God really is, and that God really answers prayer.

I recall an experience of my own that was full of blessing to me, and full of encouragement to my faith. In my first pastorate there were two persons whom God put upon my heart and for whose salvation I prayed through my entire pastorate there. But I left that field of labor without seeing either one of them converted. I went to Germany for further study, and then took a new pastorate in Minneapolis, but I kept on praying every day for those two persons. I went back to the

134

place where I began my ministry to hold a series of meetings, praying every day for the conversion of those two persons. Then one night in that series of meetings, when I gave out the invitation for all who would accept the Lord Jesus Christ as their personal Savior, those two people arose side by side. There was no special reason why they should be side by side, for they were not relatives. Oh, and when I saw those two persons for whom I had prayed every day through all those years standing up side by side to accept the Lord Jesus Christ, what an overwhelming sense came over my soul that there is a God, and that He hears prayer if we meet the conditions of prevailing prayer, and follow the method of prevailing prayer taught in His own Word.

We find right here why it is that many prayers fail of accomplishing that which we seek from God. We pray and pray and pray, and are almost on the verge of the attainment of that for which we are praying, and right then, when God is just about to answer the prayer, we stop and we miss the blessing. For example, in many churches and in many communities there are people who are praying for a revival, and the revival does not come at once, it does not come for some time, and they keep on praying. They have nearly prayed through, they are right on the verge of attaining what they sought, and if they prayed a little longer the revival would have broken upon them. But they get discouraged, throw up their hands, and quit. Just on the border of the blessing, but they do not cross into the promised land. One January, the faculty of the Bible Institute of Chicago instituted a late prayer-meeting Saturday nights from nine to ten o'clock, to pray for a world-wide revival. After we had been praying for some time the thing happened that I knew would happen when we began; people came to me, or to my colleague who was most closely identified with me in the conduct of these meetings, and they asked, "Has the revival come?"

"No, not as far as we can see."

"When is it coming?"

"We don't know."

"How long are you going to pray?"

"Until it comes." And come it did, a revival that

135

began there in that prayer-meeting room of the Bible Institute in Chicago and then broke out in far-away China, and Japan, and Australia, and New Zealand, Tasmania, and India, and swept around the world, with most marvelous manifestations of God's saving power, not merely through Mr. Alexander and myself, but through a multitude of others in India and Wales and elsewhere. In Wales, for example, under Evan Roberts and others, it resulted in 100,000 professed conversions in twelve months. And I believe that God is looking to us today to pray through again.

I prayed fifteen long years for the conversion of my oldest brother. He seemed to be getting farther and farther away from any hope of conversion, but I prayed on, and one morning, my first winter in Chicago, after fifteen years of praying, never missing a single day, God said to me as I knelt in prayer, "I have heard your prayer. You need not pray any more, your brother is going to be converted." And within two weeks my brother was in my home, shut in with sickness which made it impossible for him to leave my home, shut in for two weeks, and then the day he left he accepted Christ over in the Bible Institute in Mr. Moody's office, where he and I went to talk and pray together.

I told this incident once when I was holding meetings in a certain city. An elderly woman came to me at the close of the meeting and she said, "I have been praying for the conversion of my brother, who is sixty-three years old, for many years; but, a short time ago I gave up and stopped praying; but" she added, "I am going to begin my prayers again." And within two weeks of that time she came to me and said, "I have heard from my brother and he has accepted Christ." Oh, men and women, pray through; *pray through;* PRAY THROUGH. Do not just begin to pray and pray a little while and throw up your hands and quit, but pray, and pray, and pray, until God bends the heavens and comes down.

II. *Praying in the Holy Spirit*

There is another passage closely connected with the two that we have just been studying, and that is closely connected with them *in thought,* to which I shall now call your attention. It is found in Ephesians 6:18: "With all prayer and supplication praying at all seasons *in the Spirit*, and watching thereunto in all perseverance and supplication for all the saints."

The three words to which I wish to call your attention are these, *"In the Spirit."* We find the same thought in the epistle of Jude, verses 20 and 21: "But ye, beloved, building up yourselves on your most holy faith, *praying in the Holy Ghost,* keep yourselves in the love of God, looking for the mercy of our Lord Jesus Christ unto eternal life." In those words, "praying in the Holy Spirit," and "praying in the Holy Ghost," we find one of the two greatest secrets of prevailing prayer.

The other of the two greatest secrets of prevailing prayer is found in the words of our Lord Jesus in John 14:13, 14: "And whatsoever ye shall ask *in my name,* that will I do, that the Father may be glorified in the Son. If ye shall ask any thing *in my name,* that will I do." Those words we studied before, "Praying *in the name of the Lord Jesus,"* and "Praying *in the Holy Ghost,"* are the two great secrets of prevailing prayer. If anyone should ask me, "What is the great secret of holy living," I would say at once, "Living in the Holy Spirit." If anyone should ask me, "What is the great secret of effective service for Jesus Christ," I should reply at once, "Serving in the Holy Spirit." If anyone should ask me, "What is the one greatest secret of profitable Bible study?" I would reply, "Studying in the Holy Spirit." And if anyone should ask me, what was the one great all-inclusive secret of prevailing prayer, I should reply, *"Praying in the Holy Spirit."* It is the prayer that the Holy Spirit inspires that God the Father answers.

What does it mean to pray in the Holy Ghost? To pray "in the Holy Ghost," or to "pray in the Holy Spirit," means to pray as the Holy Spirit, our ever present, indwelling Friend, Counselor, and Guide, the "other Comforter," whom our Lord Jesus Himself promised us when He Himself left this world (John 14:15-17, 26), and who has taken the place of our Lord during His absence from us, inspires us and guides us to pray. Over and over again as we have studied together we have seen our dependence upon the Holy Spirit if we are to pray aright. When we were studying Acts 12:5 in our chapter, "How to pray so as to get what we ask," we saw it was the Holy Spirit, whose work it was to lead us into the presence of God and to make God real to us, so that we were really praying "unto God"; we saw also that it was He who gave us that intense earnestness in prayer that prevails with God. And when we were studying how to pray "according to the will of God," and how to pray "the prayer of faith," we saw that it was the Holy Spirit who revealed to us what God's will was as we prayed, and who led us to pray according to His will so that we might know as we prayed that we had asked something that was according to God's will, and might know that the prayer was heard.

1. *What are the characteristics of the prayer that is "in the Holy Spirit," the characteristics of the praying which the Holy Spirit inspires?*

(1) *The first characteristic of the prayer that is in the Holy Spirit is intense earnestness.* This we see in Romans 8:26: "And in like manner the Spirit also helpeth our infirmity: for we know not how to pray as we ought; but the Spirit himself maketh intercession for us *with groanings which cannot be uttered.*"

As we saw in studying Acts 12:5, the prayer that prevails with God is the prayer into which we throw our whole heart, the prayer of intense earnestness; and it is the Holy Spirit who inspires us to that intense earnestness in prayer. Oh, how cold and formal we are in many of our prayers. How little intense longing there is in our souls to obtain the thing that we ask. We pray even for the salvation of the lost with much indifference, though we ought to realize that if our prayers are not heard they are going to spend eternity in hell. But men and women whose prayer life is under the control of the Holy Spirit, pray with intense earnestness; they cry mightily to God; there is a great burden of prayer in their hearts; they pray sometimes with groanings which cannot be uttered. Mr. Finney told us about a man named Abel Clary. He said of him, "He had been licensed to preach; but his spirit of prayer was such, he was so burdened with the souls of men, that he was not able to preach much, his whole time and strength being

138

given to prayer. The burden of his soul would frequently be so great that he was unable to stand, and he would writhe and groan in agony. I was well acquainted with him, and knew something of the wonderful spirit of prayer that was upon him. He was a very silent man, as almost all are who have that powerful spirit of prayer." Abel Clary was of great assistance to Mr. Finney, simply by praying, in his work in Rochester, N. Y., where a revival sprang up the report of which resulted in revivals all over the country, and which, it is said, brought 100,000 souls to Christ in a year.

Of Mr. Clary's work in Rochester, Mr. Finney wrote, "The first I knew of his being in Rochester, a gentleman who lived about a mile west of the city called on me one day and asked me if I knew a Mr. Abel Clary, a minister. I told him that I knew him well. 'Well,' he said, 'he is at my house, and has been there for some time, and I don't know what to think of him.' I said, 'I have not seen him at any of our meetings.' 'No,' he replied, 'he cannot go to meeting, he says. He prays nearly all the time, day and night, and in such agony of mind that I do not know what to make of it. Sometimes he cannot even stand on his knees, but will lie prostrate on the floor, and groan and pray in a manner that quite astonishes me.' I said to the brother, 'I understand it: please keep still. It will all come out right; he will surely prevail.'"

Mr. Finney said of Mr. Clary in another place, "I think it was the second Sabbath that I was at Auburn, at this time I observed in the congregation the solemn face of Mr. Clary. He looked as if he was borne down with an agony of prayer. Being well acquainted with him, and knowing the great gift of God that was upon him, the spirit of prayer, I was glad to see him there. He sat in the pew with his brother, the doctor, who was also a professor of religion, but who had nothing by experience, I should think, of his brother Abel's great power with God. At intermission, as soon as I came down from the pulpit, Mr. Clary, with his brother, met me at the pulpit stairs, and the doctor invited me to go home with him and spend the intermission and get some refreshments. I did so.

"After arriving at his house we were soon summoned to the dinner table. We gathered about the table, and Dr. Clary turned to his brother and said, 'Brother Abel, will you ask the blessing?' Brother Abel bowed his head and began, audibly, to ask a blessing. He had uttered but a sentence or two when he broke instantly down, moved suddenly back from the table, and fled to his chamber. The doctor supposed he had been taken suddenly ill, and rose up and followed him. In a few moments he came down and said, 'Mr. Finney, Brother Abel wants to see you.' Said I, 'What ails him?' Said he, 'I do not know but he says you know. He appears in great distress, but I think it is the state of his mind.' I understood it in a moment, and went to his room. He lay groaning upon the bed, the Spirit making intercession for him, and in him, with groanings that could not be uttered. I had barely entered the room when he made out to say, 'Pray, brother Finney.' I knelt down and helped him in prayer, by leading his soul out for the conversion of sinners. I continued to pray until his distress passed away, and then I returned to the dinner table." A wonderful revival broke out in Auburn; hundreds of souls were converted in six weeks.

Oh, that we had people in our churches, who knew how to pray like that. I believe that the greatest need of the church of Jesus Christ in America today, and the church of Jesus Christ throughout the world, is men and women who pray in the Holy Spirit, with the intense earnestness that He gives, and He alone gives.

(2) *The second characteristic of praying in the Holy Spirit is intelligent praying, perfect wisdom in our praying, praying for things that are according to the will of God.* This comes out in the next verse, Romans 8:27: "And he that searcheth the hearts knoweth what is the *mind of the Spirit,* because he maketh intercession for the saints according to the will of God."

(3) *The third characteristic of the praying that is really "praying in the Holy Spirit," is complete assurance that God has heard and answered our prayer.* This we saw in studying Mark 11:24, the prayer of faith. It is the prayer that the Holy Spirit inspires that is really "the prayer of faith," and the one who so prays knows that he is praying "according to the will of God" and

140

has assurance without a shadow of a doubt that God has heard and answered his prayer.

(4) The fourth characteristic of the praying that is really *"praying in the Holy Spirit" is determination in our praying, the determination to get what we ask from God, a persistence in asking until we do get it.* This comes out clearly in Ephesians 6:18, *"With all prayer* and *supplication* praying *at all seasons in the Spirit,* and *watching thereunto in all perseverance and supplication for all the saints."* What a marvelous setting forth, by a piling up of words of deepest significance, the determination and perseverance in prayer that comes from the Holy Spirit having control of our prayer life. We do not need to dwell upon that now; for we have just been talking about it in the earlier part of this chapter. Such are the characteristics of the praying that is really in the Holy Spirit.

2. We come now to the intensely practical question, and the immediately important question, *"How may we pray in the Holy Spirit?* That is, how can we make sure that the Spirit of God is guiding us in our prayer, make sure that our prayers are not merely the promptings of our own selfish desires but the sure leadings of the Spirit of God within us? The answer to this all-important question is plainly set forth in the Word of God.

(1) First of all, *If we are to pray in the Spirit, we must surrender our wills and ourselves absolutely and unreservedly to God.* This comes out in many places in Scripture. For example, in Acts 5:32 we read: "And we are witnesses of these things; and so is the Holy Spirit, whom God hath given *to them that obey him."* Here we are plainly taught that God gives the Holy Spirit "to them that obey Him," and to them only; and the heart of obedience is in the will, the surrender of the will and the surrender of one's self to God. Unless we make this absolute surrender God cannot take control of our lives by His Holy Spirit, and He cannot take control of our prayer life any more than any other part of our life. Our surrender to Him must extend to our praying as well as to the other spheres of our activities.

(2) In the second place. *If we would pray in the Holy Spirit, we must scrupulously obey God in every*

department of our lives. Disobedience at any point of our life grieves the Holy Spirit and makes it impossible for Him to control us in our actions, and it is just as impossible for Him to take control of our prayer life as it is to take charge of any other part of our life.

To obey God we must study the Word of God every day of our lives to find out what the will of God is, and then whenever we find it, do it every time. If we refuse to do it at any point the Holy Spirit cannot keep control of our prayer life, and we cannot "pray in the Holy Spirit." That comes out very clearly in John 14:13, 14: "And whatsoever ye shall ask in my name, that will I do, that the Father may be glorified in the Son. If ye shall ask anything in my name, that will I do." And then Jesus went on to say, and by saying it clearly showed the connection between daily obedience and that power in prayer that comes through praying in the Holy Spirit, "If ye love me, ye will keep my commandments. And I will pray the Father, and *he shall give you another Comforter,* that he may be with you for ever, even the Spirit of truth, whom the world cannot receive; for it beholdeth him not, neither knoweth him: ye know him; for he abideth with you, and shall be in you."

In other words, the Lord Jesus says that if we have that love to Him that leads us to obey Him in everything, day by day, then He prays the Father and the Father sends His Holy Spirit to help us in all the emergencies of life, especially in our prayer life. Thus whatsoever we ask in His name is "according to His will," and, therefore, whatsoever we ask we get. Oh, how we come again and again and again in our study of all these wonderful promises of God to answer prayer upon the thought that *there is no effective praying of any kind possible on our part unless we are studying the Word of God daily to find out the will of God and doing it every time we find it.*

(3) In the third place, *if we would pray in the Holy Spirit we must realize and keep in mind our own utter inability to pray aright, and our entire dependence upon the Holy Spirit, if we are to pray wisely and prevailingly.* Oh, if there is any time when we need to feel our utter dependence upon the Comforter, the ever

142

present Friend and Helper and Counselor, the Holy Spirit, it is when we pray. We need to feel deeply our dependence upon Him in our living, in our daily warfare with the world, the flesh and the devil; we need to feel our dependence upon Him in our service for Christ, realizing that it is "not by might nor by power" (not by any natural gifts or abilities of our own), but "By His Spirit," that we are to accomplish anything for God in this world (Zech. 4:6); we need to feel our *dependence upon Him in our Bible study, realizing that* He is the only perfect interpreter of the Word, and that He is ready to interpret the Word to us as we study: *but above all we need to feel our dependence upon Him when we pray.* We will do well if we always bear in mind the inspired words of Paul as found in Romans 8:26, *"We know not how to pray as we ought."* If Paul, that mighty servant of Jesus Christ, that inspired apostle, that wonderful man of prayer, knew not how to pray as he ought, certainly we do not. But we should also constantly keep in mind the words that immediately follow in that same verse, and the following verse, *"But the Spirit himself maketh intercession for us* with groanings which cannot be uttered; and he that searcheth the hearts knoweth what is in the mind of the Spirit, because he maketh intercession for the saints according to the will of God." When you go to God in prayer, realize that you do not know how to pray as you ought, and bring before yourself and keep before yourself your utter dependence upon the Holy Spirit in every word of prayer.

(4) In the fourth place, *If we would pray in the Holy Spirit we must definitely ask God to guide us by His Holy Spirit as we pray.* Tell God that you do not know how to pray as you ought, and ask Him to guide you by His Spirit as you pray, and He will.

(5) In the fifth place, *If we would pray in the Holy Spirit we must count upon God's answering our prayer to send His Holy Spirit to teach us to pray; we must count upon His sending His Holy Spirit to teach us to pray.* We can unhesitatingly count upon God sending Him because in the passage just read, Romans 8:26, 27, He has definitely promised to do so.

(6) In the sixth place, *If we would pray in the Holy*

143

Spirit we must keep getting filled with the Holy Spirit.
Paul's inspired exhortation in Ephesians 5:18, "Be filled
with the Spirit," or to translate more literally, "Be
getting filled with the Holy Spirit" (it is a continuous
process, as is indicated by the tense of the Greek verb
here used), has the most intimate connection with our
prayer life. If we are filled with the Spirit we will be
guided by the Spirit in our prayers as well as in everything else. A Spirit-filled man will always be a *prayer-
ful* man, and his prayers will be in the Holy Spirit. The
way to be getting continually filled with the Holy Spirit
is indicated in what we have just studied under the four
preceding heads. If we do the things there indicated we
will be continually getting filled with the Spirit of God.

(7) Finally, *If we would pray in the Spirit we must
study the Word of God daily and earnestly.* The written
Word of God is the visible instrument through which
the invisible Spirit of God works; so if you would keep
filled with that Spirit you must keep full of the Word.
This is clearly set forth in the passage to which we have
just referred, Ephesians 5:18, when we read with it the
verse that immediately follows and then compare with
Colossians 3:16. Note Ephesians 5:18, 19: "Be filled
with the Spirit; *speaking one to another in psalms and
hymns and spiritual songs,* singing and making melody
with your heart to the Lord." Now note carefully
Colossians 3:16: "Let the *Word of Christ* dwell in you
richly; in all wisdom *teaching and admonishing one
another with psalms and hymns and spiritual songs,
singing with grace in your hearts unto God."* We see
here that Paul in Colossians attributes to being filled
with the Word exactly the same thing that he attributes
to being filled with the Spirit in Ephesians 5:18, 19, and
these two epistles were written at just about the same
time. *We must never lose sight of the tremendously
important fact that the invisible Spirit of God does His
work through the visible written Word of God. If we
keep ourselves in harmony with the mind of God by a
constant daily study of the Word of God, and by
scrupulous obedience to the Word of God, the instrument through which the Holy Spirit constantly works,
then the Holy Spirit will guide us in our prayers;* and
only then. If we keep ourselves full of the Holy Spirit's

144

truth contained in the written Word, the Holy Spirit is far more likely to pray through us. From this point of view, then, there is deepest significance in our Lord's own words found in John 6:63: *"The words that I have spoken unto you, they are Spirit, and they are life."* How often in our study of the most significant and precious passages in the Bible that bear on the subject of how to pray so as to obtain from God the things that we ask of Him in prayer, we have been brought face to face with the great truth that, *prevailing prayer always goes hand in hand with persistent and obedient study of the Word of God.*

To sum up what we have discovered on the subject of prevailing prayer: If we are to pray the prayer that obtains from our Heavenly Father the things that we ask of Him:

First of all, we must be careful as to what we ask of God, and be sure that it is something that we ought to have, something that is according to His infinitely wise and absolutely holy will, and then when we begin to pray for it to keep on praying for it for days and weeks and months, and if need be for years, until we get it. We *"ought always to pray, and not to faint." We ought to pray through.*

In the second place, we must see to it that we pray not out from our own selfish (and it may be foolish) desires, but under the impulse and inspiration and guidance and control of the Holy Spirit; that we "pray in the Holy Spirit," that we let Him pray through us and so we pray in the wisdom and earnestness and intensity and never wearying persistence and resistless power of prayer that He imparts.

Then our prayer will be the mightiest power on earth; for all God has, and all God is, is at the disposal of that kind of praying. That kind of praying can accomplish anything that God Himself can accomplish. That kind of praying partakes of the omnipotence of the God with whom that kind of praying puts us in perfect connection. I long to live in the Holy Ghost; I long to preach and witness in the Holy Ghost; I long to study and understand the Word of God in the Holy Ghost; but above all else I long to pray in the Holy

Ghost. I long also that the church as a body should learn to pray in the Holy Ghost. Then nothing shall be able to stand against the church as it sweeps on and on, from victory to victory for God.

9

HINDRANCES TO PRAYER

"Ye lust, and have not; ye kill, and covet, and cannot obtain; ye fight and war; ye have not, because ye ask not. Ye ask, and receive not, because ye ask amiss, that ye may spend it in your pleasures."—JAMES 4:2, 3, R.V.

Why it is that God sometimes does not answer the prayers of His children? James 4:2, 3 explains: "Ye lust, and have not: ye kill, and covet, and cannot obtain: ye fight and war; ye have not, because ye ask not. Ye ask, and receive not, *because ye ask amiss,* that ye may spend it in your pleasures."

In the second verse we are told that the reason why we do not have the things that we earnestly desire and urgently need is because we do not ask for them, because we do not pray: we are told that "Ye have not, *because ye ask not."* The secret of our poverty and powerlessness is neglect of prayer. We may put forth the most strenuous activity to get things that we need— lust, kill, covet, fight and war—and yet fail to get them because we do not pray. In studying this verse earlier we saw clearly that the great secret of the poverty and powerlessness of the average Christian, the average minister, and the average church, was neglect of prayer. But in the third verse we are told that we may pray and still not obtain, because "Ye ask amiss," or, as the Greek word translated "amiss" means, "Ask evilly, wrongly, or improperly"; that is to say, that there is something that hinders God from answering our prayers.

As we have discussed the mighty power of prayer, and the great and wonderful things prayer brings to pass, many may have said to themselves, "Well, my prayers have no such power as that. God doesn't hear and answer my prayers that way." Why is that? Is it because what the Bible teaches about prayer is not true? Is it because God does not answer prayer? Is it because God in olden times answered prayer but does not answer it any longer? No, not at all. It is for none of those reasons. Why is it then? It is because there is something in your own life, or in your heart, that makes it impossible for God to answer your prayers. It is because there is something in your case that HINDERS PRAYER.

Now we are to study what these hindrances to prayer are, what the things are in our hearts, or in our lives, that make it impossible for God to answer our prayers. And I trust that when you see what the things are that prevent God answering your prayers, you will give them up and thus get into a place where you can not only pray but also obtain.

I. *A Wrong Motive in Our Prayers*

The first hindrance to prayer you will find right in our text: "Ye ask, and receive not, because ye ask amiss, *that ye may consume it upon your lusts.*" The Revised Version reads a little differently and more correctly, "Ye ask, and receive not, because ye ask amiss, that ye may *spend it in your pleasures." The first thing, then, that hinders prayers, the first thing that makes it impossible for God to answer our prayers, is a selfish purpose in our prayers.* We ask for things we have a right to ask for, things that it is the will of God to give us, but we ask for them in a wrong way; that is, we ask from a wrong motive, we ask for them for our own selfish gratification, that (as the Bible puts it) we "may spend it in our pleasures."

What ought to be our motive in our prayers? The Bible answers that question plainly and explicitly in I Corinthians 10:31, "Whether therefore ye eat, or drink, or whatsoever ye do, *do all to the glory of God." Here* we are told distinctly that in everything we do, even in

148

our eating and drinking, the glory of God should be our main object in going it. If that is true of the simplest duties of everyday life, it certainly must be true of our praying. *Our supreme motive in our prayers should be that God may be glorified by answering our prayers;* not that we may get some gratification, but that God may get glory to Himself. This thought comes out again and again in the Bible. For example, the Lord Jesus said in John 14:13, in that wonderful promise we have quoted so often, "And whatsoever ye shall ask in my name, that will I do, *that the Father may be glorified in the Son."* Then in that prayer that our Lord Himself taught us, as recorded in the sixth chapter of Matthew, the prayer begins with these words, "Our Father which art in heaven, *hallowed be thy name,"* clearly showing us that the first thing in our prayers should be the hallowing of God's own name, the glorifying of God Himself. Then again in John 17:1, that marvelous prayer that our Lord Jesus offered the night before His crucifixion, the real "Lord's prayer," our Lord began with these words, "Father, the hour is come; glorify thy Son, *that thy Son also may glorify thee."* Whatever we ask of God in prayer, the first great purpose we have in asking anything should be that God may be glorified in giving it. But that this is far from the thought of many of us when we pray will be evident from a few simple illustrations.

For example, how many a Christian woman is praying for the conversion of her husband? Now that certainly is a proper thing to pray for; indeed, I cannot see how any truly coverted woman can rest, or give God rest day or night, until her husband is truly converted and born again. But as proper as that prayer is, it often fails because the wife who offers it is praying for the conversion of her husband from a purely selfish motive. She thinks to herself, "How much happier our married life would be if both my husband and I were Christians; then we would sympathize in the deepest interests in life, and we would know what real marriage means." Now that is all true. No two persons can know the deepest joys of married life, and the real meaning of true marriage, where one is saved and the other unsaved; where one is "a believer" and the other is "an unbeliever." But to pray for the conversion of your husband for that reason is pure selfishness; a refined selfishness it is true, but nevertheless selfishness.

Or a woman often prays for the conversion of her husband because she cannot bear the thought that *her* husband should be lost forever. That, too, is pure selfishness; refined selfishness, but nevertheless selfishness. Why should a wife pray for the conversion of her husband? First of all, and above all else, that God may be glorified in the conversion of her husband; because she cannot bear it that God should any longer be dishonored by the Christless, godless, God-disobeying life of her husband; that God may be glorified by her husband obeying God and doing the first thing that God demands of every man, believe on His Son the Lord Jesus Christ; that God may be glorified in her husband ceasing his rebellion against God and his wicked life, and giving himself up to Jesus Christ and His service; that should be the supreme motive for which a Christian woman prays for the conversion of her husband. And when a woman gets to praying for the conversion of her husband along that line, it will not be long before she sees him converted.

How far that is from the thought of many a woman who is praying most earnestly, and even agonizingly, for the conversion of her husband, however, that is very evident from the way in which she speaks to you about her husband. She will come to you and say, "I wish you would pray for my husband that he may be converted; he is *such a good man*. It is true he is not a Christian, but he is such a good man." Could any woman who had any proper conception of the infinite majesty and glory of God, or the divine majesty and dignity of His Son, Jesus Christ, call a man, no matter how kind he might be to her and just to others, "a *good* man" when he is disobeying God in the very first thing that God demands of him, that he believe in His Son Jesus Christ? When he is trampling under foot the glorious Son of God; calling such a man "a good man" just because he is her husband? No, no, no, he may be your husband, he may be kind and generous and excellent in many ways, but if he is rejecting Jesus Christ he is a wicked, stubborn, rebel against God. You may love

150

him, you ought to love him, but do not dishonor God by calling him *good;* but cry to God for His conversion not merely that you may have the joy of seeing him converted, and not merely that he may have the joy of being converted and be saved from an eternal hell, but in order that God may be glorified in his conversion. Pray that way and it will not be long before you see your husband converted.

Take another illustration. Many a minister, and many a professing Christian, is praying for a true revival. That certainly is a proper prayer; that certainly is a prayer that is according to God's will; it is a Bible prayer, for we read in Psalm 85:6 this prayer: "Wilt thou not revive us again: that thy people may rejoice in thee?" Yes, that is a perfectly proper prayer; indeed, I cannot see how anyone who is a real Christian can keep from praying that prayer with intense earnestness in days such as these. But one may, and men often do, offer that prayer from an entirely selfish motive. Many a minister is praying for a revival in his church from a purely selfish motive. I received a letter once from a minister, the pastor of a church, beseeching me to come and hold a meeting with him, and he wrote, "I am losing my hold upon my people, and if I do not have a revival I will have to give up my church." In other words, he wanted a revival merely that he might hold his living. That perhaps was an extreme case, but there are many that are essentially the same; both ministers and members praying for a revival that there may be an increase of members in the church; that the church may have a larger prestige in the community; in the hope sometimes that some of the rich people in the community may be converted and so the burden of supporting the church will not be so heavy upon them, or for many other purely selfish reasons.

Why ought we to pray for a revival? That God may be glorified by a revival; because we can no longer bear it that God should be dishonored by the low level of living among professed Christians, and by the increase of wickedness and godlessness in the world; because we can no longer endure it that God should be dishonored by the outspoken infidelity so common among men today, and by the even more dangerous infidelity of

151

many of our church members, and even of some alleged preachers of the Gospel today; that God may be glorified by the church being brought up to that level of Christian life that will glorify God, and by the conversion of sinners, and by stopping the mouths of unbelievers, and by delivering some of our church members and our preachers from dangerous heresy and unbelief to a God-honoring faith in God's Word and the truth contained in His Word. That God may be glorified; that is why we should pray for a revival. But how far that is from the thought of many who are praying for a revival today.

Take still another illustration. There are a great many ministers and members in our churches today who are praying that they may be baptized with the Holy Spirit. That is certainly a proper prayer, a prayer that pleases God, a prayer that has abundant warrant in the Word of God, for the Lord Jesus distinctly tells us in Luke 11:13, "If ye then, being evil, know how to give good gifts unto your children; how much more shall your heavenly Father give the Holy Spirit *to them that ask him?*" And we read in the record in Acts 4:31, "And when they had prayed, the place was shaken where they were assembled together; and they were all filled with the Holy Ghost, and they spake the word of God with boldness." Yes, indeed, it is a proper prayer; and I cannot understand how any Christian can rest until he is baptized with the Holy Spirit, and knows it. But there is much prayer for the baptism with the Holy Spirit, or the filling with the Holy Spirit, which is purely selfish. Men and women pray for the baptism with the Holy Spirit because they think they will be happier if they are thus baptized. They know men and women who have been baptized with the Holy Spirit, and such a new and radiant and glorious joy has come into their lives that they want it, too. Or, it may be that they pray for the baptism with the Holy Spirit because they know someone else who has been baptized with the Holy Spirit and a new power has come into their service, and they want the baptism with the Holy Spirit that they, too, may be more prominent and successful in their work for God. Now all this is pure selfishness, and one can pray for the baptism with the Holy Spirit in that way until the crack of doom and never obtain it.

Why should we desire the baptism with the Holy Spirit? Or why, if we have been baptized with the Holy Spirit, should we pray for a new filling with the Holy Spirit? That God may be glorified in our being baptized or filled with the Holy Spirit. Because we can no longer endure it that God should be any longer dishonored by the low level of our living, and by the ineffectiveness of our service; that God may be glorified by our being empowered to lead such lives as honor Him; that God may be glorified by our having the power in His service that we ought to have; that God may be glorified by our being baptized or filled with the Holy Spirit—that is why we should pray for it. And when we get to praying for the baptism with the Holy Spirit along that line it will not be many hours before we are thus baptized with the Spirit of God. But how far this is from the thought of many who are praying for the baptism with the Holy Spirit is very evident from the way they talk, and the way they pray.

A friend of mine was holding a meeting in a town in New York State, near the Hudson River. At one of his morning services he spoke upon the baptism with the Holy Spirit. As he went away from the meeting one of the ministers of the town walked with him. They had not gone far when this minister said, "I greatly enjoyed your address this morning. The baptism of the Holy Spirit that you were talking about is just what I need, and that is what I am going to have." Now that sounded encouraging, but the minister went on to say, "I have a salary of twelve thousand dollars a year. I believe if I had that baptism of the Holy Spirit that you have been talking about I could get fifteen thousand dollars a year." Now you smile at that, but it is really shocking, indeed appalling. It may be an extreme case, but it illustrates a tendency of thought that is exceedingly common among professed Christians and among ministers today who are praying that they may be baptized with the Holy Spirit, or that they may be filled with the Holy Spirit. Oh, brethren, when you and I come to see this thing in the Bible light, come to see how God-dishonoring our lives are, and come to long for the baptism with the Holy Spirit, or filling with the

Holy Spirit, not that *we* may be *blessed,* but that God may be *glorified,* it will not be long before we are baptized with the Holy Ghost.

II. *Sin in the Heart or Life*

You will find a second hindrance to prayer set forth in Isaiah 59:1, 2: "Behold, the Lord's hand is not short-ened, that it cannot save: neither his ear heavy, that it cannot hear: But your iniquities have separated between you and your God, and your sins have hid his face from you, that he will not hear." Here we are distinctly told that in many instances the reason why God does not answer prayer is because our iniquities and our sins have separated between us and our God, and hid His face from us, that He will not hear. The people of Isaiah's time were saying, "God does not answer prayer any longer. He may have answered it in the days of Moses; He may have answered in the days of Elijah, but He does not answer any longer. Either His ear is heavy, that it cannot hear; or His hand is shortened that it cannot save."

"No, no," says Isaiah, "the Lord's hand is not short-ened, that it cannot save: neither his ear heavy, that it cannot hear." The trouble is not with God, the trouble is with you. *"Your iniquities* have separated between you and your God, and *your sins* have hid his face from you, that he will not hear." Sin in our hearts or lives makes it impossible for God to answer our prayer, even though the thing for which we are praying is entirely according to His will.

If you are praying for something and you do not get it, do not conclude that God does not answer prayer; do not conclude that God does not answer prayer today as He did in the olden times; do not conclude that this thing that you are asking for is not according to the will of God. Go alone with God, ask Him to search your heart, and ask Him to show you whether there is any-thing in your past life that you have done that was wrong that you have not set straight, any past sin that you have not judged, or whether there is anything in your life today that is displeasing to Him. And then wait silently before Him and give Him an opportunity

154

to show you. And if He shows you anything, confess it to Him as sin and give it up.

If you will not do this, then there is not the least use in your trying to pray; nothing will come of your prayers; and it will not be because God does not hear prayer today just as much as in former days; it is not because the arm of the Lord is shortened that He cannot save, nor His ear heavy, that He cannot hear. God's ear is just as sharp to hear the voice of true prayer as it ever was, and His hand is just as long and just as strong to save as it ever was, "But *your* iniquities have separated between you and your God, and *your* sins have hid his face from you, that he will not hear." Right at this point we find the full explanation of why it is that many of our prayers are not heard and bring nothing to pass.

I had a striking illustration of this in my own life some years ago, an experience which I have never forgotten. I had started out to carry on the work that God had given me to do in Minneapolis without any pledges for its support, and without taking up any contributions or collections of any kind, but simply looking to God by prayer to furnish the money for the work. I do not believe that God asks every man to do that, or even that He asks the same man always to do it, but I was entirely sure that God had told me to do it at that time, and I had stepped out in simple faith in God. I had had a strong society behind me who paid me a generous salary, paid for the rent of the various halls, paid for the missionaries I employed, paid for all the work that was done; but I saw that the time had come when I should step out in simple faith in Him, and so I asked the society that had been supporting me if they would turn the work over to me to carry it on in that way. I told them what they knew to be true, that there was a great deal of other work they ought to be doing and they needed their money for that other work. Somewhat reluctantly but very kindly they acceded to my request, and in a single day I cut off every source of income I had in the world. From that time every penny that came for the support of myself and wife and our four children, every penny that came for rent of halls, lights, fuel, and everything else, every penny that came for my missionaries, came in answer to prayer. We took up no collections, had no subscriptions, no one was ever asked for money, no one but God. A great many people were watching the experiment, many of them very sympathetically, others possibly quite critically (though I must say that for an experiment that must have seemed to an outsider so crazy it was received, as far as I know, with kindness everywhere).

The money came in day after day, and week after week, and month after month; not from the old sources, almost entirely from new sources. Sometimes it came in small amounts; sometimes in large amounts; sometimes it came in ways most ordinary, and sometimes in ways apparently very extraordinary. But it came. But one day it did not come, that is to say, I had obligations that I must meet very soon and no money to meet them. When I went home that night, before I retired, I took the matter to God in prayer and asked Him to send me that money, not only that the work might go on, but that His name might not be dishonored by an apparent failure on His part to answer prayer. But I went to bed, I am afraid, without much clear faith that the money would come. I was all alone in the house. In the middle of the night I was awakened by great pain and physical distress; I was very sick. I looked up to God and cried to Him that He would touch my body and heal me, and that He would send that money; but there was no answer. Again I cried to God to touch my body and send that money. Still no answer. It seemed as though the heavens above my head were brass; it seemed as if there were no God there, and the devil came and taunted me. He said, as he said to the Psalmist of old, "Where is thy God? There is no God, or if there is a God He does not answer prayer in the way which you have been teaching people that He does."

I was in great distress of soul as well as body; it seemed as if the very billows of hell were going over my head; it seemed as if the cherished faith of years was going by the board. Have you ever been there? Have you ever been where it seemed the faith which you cherished for years, and that you thought was so well founded, was going by the board? Well, that was where I was. And again I cried to God. "Touch my body, heal me, and send that money." No answer. Then I looked up and I said, "Heavenly Father, if there is anything wrong in my life anywhere, show me what it is and I will give it up." Instantly God brought up something that had often come up before to trouble me, but every time it would come up I would say, "That's all right. I know it's all right. There is nothing wrong about that," but all the time in the bottom of my heart I knew it was wrong. Have you anything of that kind in your heart and life, something that always comes up when you get nearest to God to trouble you, and yet which you try to persuade yourself is right? You say to yourself, "That's all right. I know it's all right. I am sure it is all right, it is all nonsense to think that that is wrong." Well, so it was with me. It came up again vividly and I looked up and said, "Oh, God, if this thing is wrong in Thy sight, I will give it up now." No answer. In the depths of my heart I knew it was wrong, but I said, "Oh, God, *if* it is wrong in Thy sight I will give it up." There was no answer. Then I cried, "Oh, God, this thing is wrong; it is sin. I give it up now." Instantly God touched my body, immediately I was as well as I am this moment, and the money came in and the work went on.

When? When I judged my sin. Oh, men and women, if you are praying, praying, praying for something and not getting it, I beg you, do not fancy that God does not answer prayer; do not decide that the thing that you are praying for is not according to God's will! God may be dealing with you, may be trying to bring you to your senses and to Himself. Go alone with God and honestly ask Him to show you if there is anything wrong in your heart or life, anything that is displeasing to Him; and when He shows you, set it straight at once and you will find an open Heaven, and a God who answers prayer, a God whose ear is not only quick to hear prayer in general, and whose hand is not only strong to save in general, but a God whose ear is quick to hear your prayer, and whose hand is long and strong to give immediate deliverance to you. Oh, how many things there are that we greatly need and that we might have at once if we would only judge and put away our sin!

III. *Idols in the Heart*

Now turn to Ezekiel 14:1-3, where we will find a third hindrance to prayer. "Then came certain of the elders of Israel unto me, and sat before me. And the word of the Lord came unto me, saying, Son of man, these men have set up their idols in their heart, and put the stumbling-block of their iniquity before their face: should I be inquired of at all by them?" The elders of Israel had come to Ezekiel to pray for them; it was seemingly a day of great triumph for Ezekiel. For a long time, for days and months, perhaps for years, Ezekiel had been longing for the time when the elders of Israel would come to their senses and come to him and ask him to pray for them, and the time seemed to have come. With a glad heart Ezekiel was about to go to God in prayer for them, and for the people. But God suddenly stops him, He says, "Ezekiel, do not pray for these men, *they have set up their idols in their heart,* and put the stumbling-block of their iniquity before their face: *should I be inquired of at all by them?*" Here we are clearly told that *idols in the heart make it impossible for God to attend to our prayers.*

In Japan, China, and India and other non-Christian lands they set up their idols in their temples and in their homes, but the Jews, and we Christians also to-day, set up our idols in our hearts. There are no hideous images on our mantels or in other places in our homes, but there are idols in the hearts of many of us which make it just as impossible for God to answer our prayers as if we had the most hideous images in our homes or in our churches.

What is an idol? An idol is anything that a man puts before God. Many a man makes an idol of his wife. No man can love his wife too much; the more truly a man loves God, the more deeply and tenderly he will love his wife, but a man may put his wife in the wrong place, he may put his wife before God. Many a man, many a professing Christian man, many an active Christian man, does things to please his wife that he knows do not please God. He is making an idol of his wife; he is not on praying ground. Many a wife also makes an idol of her husband. No wife can love her

158

husband too much. The more truly a woman loves God, the more deeply and tenderly she will love her husband, but a wife can put her husband in the wrong place, she can put her husband before God, and she can do things to please her husband that she knows do not please God. How many a wife is doing it in these days; how many a wife is doing things in the matter of dress, in the matter of social engagements, in the matter of amusements, and in other matters, to please her husband that she knows full well in her heart do not please God. She is making an idol of her husband, and she is not on praying ground.

We can make idols of our children. We must not love our children too much; the more truly we love God, the more deeply and tenderly we will love our children, but we can put our children in the wrong place; we can put our children before God, and we can do things to please our children that we know do not please God. How many Christians are doing that very thing today? How many Christian fathers and mothers are allowing forms of amusement and social entertainment, and other things in their homes, that they know are displeasing to God, but their children want them? They are making idols of their children, and they are not on praying ground. How many a professedly Christian father and mother have a beautiful daughter for whom they are seeking a brilliant match with a man of wealth or culture or social position, and the man whom they are cultivating as a prospective husband for their Christian daughter is not a Christian man. He is gifted, he is talented, he is rich perhaps, very likely he has a delightful personality, but he is not a Christian; and, in spite of the fact that they know perfectly well that God commands in the most unmistakable terms in II Corinthians 6:14 "Be ye not unequally yoked together with unbelievers," (and by unbelievers here is not meant infidels, but unbelievers in the New Testament sense as including all who have not believed on Jesus Christ with a living faith, believed on Him with the faith that receives Him as Savior and Lord). Knowing this, in deliberate violation of God's written law, they are seeking this brilliant match for their daughter. They have made an idol of their daughter and her future prosperity and prospects. They are not on praying ground.

Many make idols of social position. How many professedly Christian men and women there are, quite earnest men and women in some respects, who are doing things to secure or maintain a social position that they desire to occupy, which they know are not right in the sight of God. Major Whittle, the evangelist, was once holding meetings in the city of Washington, D.C. An old friend of his was at the time occupying a high position in the United States Government. This friend invited Major Whittle to his beautiful Washington home. One day he was showing Major Whittle about the home, and as they went from room to room they came into a very large and beautifully decorated room. Major Whittle glanced around it and then said to the man, "What is this room for?" The man evaded an answer, but Major Whittle was not a man easily put off, and he repeated his question, "What is this room for?" The man replied, "Well, Major, if you must know, it is a ballroom." Major Whittle looked at him sternly and said, "Do you mean to tell me that you have fallen so low in the moral scale that you have a ballroom in your home?" The man dropped his head and said, "Major, I did not think I would ever come to this, but here we are in Washington society and my wife and daughter told me that we must do this to maintain our position in society, and I have yielded to them." He and his wife had made an idol of social position, and right dearly did he pay for it before he got through, and right dearly did she pay for it.

The temptation to make an idol of our reputation is peculiarly real with ministers of the Gospel. We ministers know perfectly well that in this day in which we are living, which puts such an extraordinary and absurd value upon what it calls advanced thought and original thinking, that if a minister is true to the old God-given doctrines, no matter how scholarly and how brilliant he may be, he will be by a great many persons rated as not scholarly and not up-to-date. Yet, on the other hand, no matter how little a scholar a man be, or how poor a thinker he may be, if he throws out views that are a little off color, or a great deal off color, he will at

160

once be rated as "a great thinker," as fully abreast of the times, a great scholar. So many a minister who really is perfectly sound at heart in his own views, will throw out a little suggestion now and then to make people realize that he is abreast of the times, that will under- mine the faith of the young men and young women in his congregation. He has made an idol of his reputa- tion, and lost his power in prayer. Or again, we minis- ters often realize that if we use ornate rhetoric, and theatrical modes of address, we will not win so many souls to Christ as we will by preaching the simple, straight Gospel, but we will get a far greater reputation as pulpit orators; and many a man in the pulpit today has sacrificed his real power for God by cultivating an elaborate and highly polished rhetoric and oratorical methods of delivery that awakened the admiration and applause of shallow men and women, but robbed him of real power for God. Such men have made an idol of their reputation and are not on praying ground.

Oh, if you covet power in prayer, go alone with God and let Him search you; ask Him to show you if there is any idol in your heart, and when He shows it to you, do away with it today.

> The dearest idol I have known,
>   Whate'er that idol be,
> Help me to tear it from its throne
> And worship only Thee.

IV. *An Unforgiving Spirit*

Our Lord Jesus Christ sets forth a fourth hindrance to prayer in Mark 11:25, "And when ye stand praying, forgive, if ye have aught against any; that your Father also which is in heaven may forgive you your trespass- es." Here we are distinctly told that *an unforgiving spirit makes it impossible for God to answer our prayers. All of God's answering our prayers is upon the* basis of God's dealing with us as forgiven sinners, and God cannot deal with us as forgiven sinners while we are not forgiving those who have wronged us. I believe we touch here upon one of the most frequent causes of unanswered prayer, bitterness in our heart toward someone who has wronged us, or whom we fancy has wronged us. How many a wife is praying, praying earnestly, praying with an almost breaking heart, for the conversion of her husband, but all the time she has bitterness in her heart toward someone who has wronged her, or whom she fancies has wronged her? Woman, are you willing that your husband should be eternally lost for the poor, miserable gratification of hating someone who has wronged you, or whom you fancy has wronged you? How many a mother is praying, praying so earnestly, for the conversion of her son, and all the time that she is praying for the conversion of her son she has bitter hatred in her heart toward some other woman who has wronged her, or whom she fancies has wronged her? Woman, are you willing that your son should go down to an eternal hell for the poor, miserable gratification of hating someone? If we wish power in prayer, let us search our hearts today, and let us look to God to search our hearts and bring to light any enmity that there may be in our heart toward anyone, and if we find that there is such enmity, no matter how much that person may have wronged us, let us give it up and let the Spirit of God come into our hearts, that Spirit who makes us love everyone, even our cruelest enemy.

When Mr. Alexander and I were holding meetings in Launceston, Tasmania, we had a day of fasting and prayer. There was an active Christian man in the community who had a son-in-law, and he and his wife had had some trouble with that son-in-law. They had forbidden his ever coming under their roof again. At the morning service I spoke, as I always did on the day of fasting and prayer, on hindrances to prayer. When I reached this part of my sermon the man was deeply convicted of that sin. As he went away from the meeting to his home at the noon hour he began thinking of it, and he wondered to himself whether he ought to write his son-in-law. Just as he was reaching home he was wondering whether he ought to speak to his wife about this matter. He went up the steps, reached out his hand to open the door, still thinking about this. Unknown to him, his wife had been at the meeting also, and as he reached out to open the door his wife opened the door from the other side and instantly said, "Telegraph him to come at once." And they did. And power in prayer came into the life of that man and woman. There are some reading these words who have had no power in prayer for days, or weeks, or months, or it may be for years, simply because of some bitterness that they have in their heart toward someone. There is no use whatever of your praying until you let God cast out that bitterness. Listen again to the words of Jesus Christ Himself, "When ye stand praying, forgive, if ye have aught against any; that your Father also which is in heaven may forgive you your trespasses."

V. *Stinginess in Our Giving*

Now turn to a deeply significant passage of Scripture that throws great light on the subject that we are studying, Proverbs 21:13, "Whoso stoppeth his ears at the cry of the poor, he also shall cry himself, but shall not be heard." Here God distinctly tells us that if we stop our ears to the cry of the poor when they cry unto us for help, He will stop His ears to us when we cry unto Him for help. The one who is small, and mean, and stingy, and niggardly in his giving, cannot be a mighty man of prayer. This thought runs all through the Bible. We are told it over and over again. Read, for example, Luke 6:38, "Give, and it shall be given unto you; good measure, pressed down, and shaken together, and running over, shall men give into your bosom. For with the same measure that ye mete withal it shall be measured to you again."

Here God distinctly tells us that He measures out His benefactions to us in exactly the same measure that we measure out our benefactions to others. And some of us use such tiny measures in our giving that God can only give us a pint cup blessing. God puts His gifts into our lives in answer to our prayers through the same door that we give out our benevolences to others, and some of us open the door of our benevolences such a wee crack that God can only get in the smallest blessing to us.

There is another passage, one of the most familiar promises in the Bible, a promise that one hears in almost every prayer-meeting that he attends, and yet a promise that is constantly quoted without any reference whatever to the connection and to the condition of fulfillment implied in the connection. Philippians 4:19, "But my God shall supply all your need according to his riches in glory by Christ Jesus." What a wonderful promise it is, but the English Revised Version makes it even more wonderful. "And my God shall *fulfil*," turn that word 'fulfil' around and you get exactly what the Greek word signifies 'fill full': let me read it that way, "And my God shall *fill full every need* of yours according to his riches in glory in Christ Jesus."

One of the elders of our church in Chicago stood up one night in our prayer-meeting and said, "I thank God, brethren, that there is one promise in the Bible without any condition"; and then he quoted this passage, "But my God shall supply all your need according to his riches in glory by Christ Jesus."

I stopped him and said, "Hold on a minute, Brother H——, there is a condition; it is exceedingly plain in the context. Please begin back at the fifteenth verse. Listen, 'Now ye Philippians know also, that in the beginning of the gospel, when I departed from Macedonia, no church communicated with me as concerning giving and receiving, but ye only. For even in Thessalonica ye sent once and again unto my necessity." And then he goes on to say how they had just sent to him again, and then it is that he says, "But my God shall fulfil every need of *yours* (that is, "every need of" a generously giving church) according to his riches in glory by Christ Jesus." There is absolutely nothing here that a stingy Christian has a right to claim. We are plainly told that the promise is made to large givers, and to them alone. Of course the gift may not be large in itself, but large in comparison with what a person has.

There is another familiar promise that sounds much like this one that we have just noted, II Corinthians 9:8, "And God is able to make all grace abound toward you; that ye, always having all sufficiency in all things, may abound to every good work." Just look at the "all's," and the "every's" and the "abound's." Read it again, "And God is able to make *all* grace *abound*

164

toward you; that ye, *always* having *all sufficiency* in *all* things, may *abound* to *every* good work." Wonderful promise, isn't it? But read it in its context. Begin at verses 6 and 7, "He which soweth sparingly [the context shows that Paul is speaking about the sowing of gifts, and sowing sparingly means giving sparingly] shall reap also sparingly; and he which soweth bountifully shall reap also bountifully. Every man according as he purposeth in his heart, so let him give; not grudgingly, or of necessity: for God loveth a cheerful giver (the Greek word here translated "cheerful" is "hilaros," from which we get our word "hilarious"). And God is able to make all grace abound toward *you* (that is, toward the hilarious giver); that ye (that is, that ye hilarious givers), always having all sufficiency in all things may abound to every good work."

There is nothing here for the stingy Christian, only for the Christian who is a hilarious giver. Are you a hilarious giver? Do you love to find opportunities to give? When you see the collection basket coming, do you say to yourself, "I am so glad I have another opportunity to give"? Or do you say, "I wish they wouldn't everlastingly take up collections"?

Take one other passage of Scripture, that wonderful promise in I John 3:22, "And whatsoever we ask, we receive of him, because we keep his commandments, and do those things that are pleasing in his sight." What a wonderful promise that is. John here tells us plainly that whatsoever he asked of God he received. But why? Read the context; begin back at the sixteenth verse, "Hereby perceive we the love of God, because he laid down his life for us: and we ought to lay down our lives for the brethren. But whoso hath this world's good, and seeth his brother have need, and shutteth up his bowels of compassion from him, how dwelleth the love of God in him?" I can tell you how—nohow! But read on, "My little children, let us not love *in word,* neither *in tongue; but in deed* and *in truth."* That is to say, let us not love in mere profession of love, but in reality, by actually doing.

For example, it is a cold winter night, there are only a few out to prayer-meeting, but an enthusiastic brother enters and in a little while he gets up in the prayer-meeting and says, "Brethren, I am so glad to be here tonight. I do so enjoy the society of Christian people. I know that I have passed from death unto life, because I love the brethren (I John 3:14.) Oh, how I love the brethren, how glad I am to be here tonight. I'd rather be here than to go to the theatre or the circus or any entertainment. I do not see how anyone who calls himself a Christian can go to places like that. There is no place I enjoy as I enjoy the prayer-meeting; no fellowship that I love as I love the fellowship of Christians. I know I have passed from death unto life, because I love the brethren." Immediately after the meeting is over, you go to this enthusiastic, glowing brother, and you say to him, "Brother Smith, I was so glad to hear your testimony tonight; it just warmed my heart. But I want to speak to you about a little matter. You know Sister Johnson. She has been through some rough times. Her husband died here a few months ago. He left her no insurance, and she is having a hard time to pay her rent and keep her family together. She lives in that little house of yours over on the other side of town, and she is afraid she cannot pay the rent this time. Can't you let her off on the rent?" And instantly this glowing Christian becomes cold, and he says, "Well, of course I sympathize with the poor sister, and I wish I could help her, but business is business, and if she cannot pay the rent I suppose she will have to get out." How dwelleth the love of God in that man? I will tell you how—nohow! He simply loves "in word" and "in tongue," not "in deed and in truth."

Take another illustration. Another brother comes into a prayer-meeting where you are present, and he gets up with the same glowing testimony, tells how glad he is to be there, how he loves the brethren, how he loves the society of Christian people, how he knows that he has passed from death unto life, because he loves the brethren. When the meeting is over you go to him and say, "Brother Brown, I so enjoyed your testimony tonight; it did me good, it warmed my heart. But, Brother Brown, you know Sister Jones, you know what a hard time she is having of it. You remember how her husband coming home from work a few weeks ago was run over by a train and killed, and how he had

166

no insurance and no money saved, and she has been unable to get any damages from the railroad. It is going to be a cold winter, and they have no coal over in Sister Jones' house, and we are getting together a little money to stock the house with coal or wood, and to put in a barrel of flour, and potatoes, and other provisions, so that she can keep her family together and not separate, and not suffer." Suddenly this brother also becomes cold and says, "Well, I am sorry for her, and I'd like to help her, but charity must begin at home. And I've got to pay my income tax, and you know how heavy it is. (It does not seem to occur to the brother that unless he had plenty of money he would not have a very heavy income tax.) And though I would like to help, I cannot."

"How dwelleth the love of God in him?" Nohow. He loves merely "in word" and "in tongue," and not "in deed and in truth." But read on, "And hereby [that is, by loving not merely in word and in tongue, but by our actual giving, "in deed and in truth"] we know that we are of the truth, and shall assure our hearts before him [that is, before God]. For if our heart condemn us, [that is, condemn us in the matter of our stingy giving], God is greater than our heart, and knoweth all things. Beloved, if our heart condemn us not [that is, does not condemn us because of our stingy giving], then have we confidence toward God. And whatsoever *we* ask [that is, we whose hearts do not condemn us because of our stinginess, we who are giving generously as we ought, we who love "in deed and in truth"] whatsoever *we* ask, we receive of him, because we keep his commandments, and do those things that are pleasing in his sight." You may go right straight through your Bible and you will find that every great promise on God's part to give us in answer to our prayer, is conditioned upon our generous giving to others who need our help.

Right here we discover the secret of why it is that individual believers, and the Church of Christ as a whole, today have so little power in prayer. It is because of our downright stinginess in giving. Great men of prayer are all great givers, that is, great givers according to their ability. George Mueller, of Bristol,

167

England, was, as far as we know, one of the greatest men of prayer of the last generation. He obtained the English equivalent of more than $7,200,000.00 by prayer. For about sixty years he carried on a most marvelous work in supporting and training the orphans of England, oftentimes housing two thousand or more orphans at one time, feeding them three meals a day. Yet every penny that came for the support of the orphans, and for the support of the other work for which he felt responsible, came in answer to prayer. No appeal was ever made to anyone, no collections or offerings were ever taken, and yet the money never failed. Sometimes it seemed up to almost the last moment as if it would fail, but it always came. He would ask God for a hundred pounds sterling, and it would come and he would pass it on. He would ask for sixty thousand pounds sterling, and it would come and he would pass it on. In all, as we have already stated, he asked for over $7,200,000.00 and it came and he passed it on.

That was the reason why it kept coming, because he kept passing it on. None of it stuck to his fingers. And when he came to die at the advanced age of ninety-two or ninety-three years, he had just enough left to pay his funeral expenses. We ask and we get and *we keep,* and so God ceases to give. We stop our ears at the cry of the poor, the poor in our own land and the poor in other lands, the spiritually poor even more than the poor in purse, and so God stops His ears to our cry, just as He told us in Proverbs 21:13 He would do.

The churches of America do not average ten cents a week per member for foreign missions, and yet we wonder why God does not hear our prayers. Many a professedly Christian woman spends every year of her life more on the single article of kid gloves than she does upon foreign missions, and yet she wonders why God does not hear her prayers. I am not saying that women should not wear gloves, but I am saying that a Christian woman should certainly give more for the work of sending the Gospel to the perishing heathen than she does on a matter of personal adornment like that. Many a professing Christian man spends more every year of his life on the unnecessary, not to say filthy and unwholesome, tobacco habit than he does

168

upon sending the Gospel to the perishing in China, and India, and Africa, and elsewhere, and yet he wonders why God does not answer his prayers. There is many and many a man in our churches today who, if you ask him for $100.00 for foreign missions, would almost faint away, and yet he spends more than fifty cents a day on cigars, and fifty cents a day would make more than $100.00 in a year. Many spend many times fifty cents a day on cigars or cigarettes, or tobacco in some form, and never dream of giving the same amount to foreign missions, and yet they wonder why God does not answer their prayers. There is no wonder about it, it is your niggardliness, your downright meanness in your giving.

A young lady once came into my office in Minneapolis. I was interested in the newsboys of Minneapolis, and so was she. I was vice-president of the Newsboys' Home, and we needed something badly for that home. I have forgotten now what it was. This young woman was the daughter of a wealthy railway magnate. Standing by my table in my office she rested her fingers upon the table and said to me, "Oh, Mr. Torrey, we must get that money for the newsboys. How shall we get it?" And as she said it the value of one diamond alone that flashed on her finger would have met the need many times over.

An enthusiastic missionary advocate at a great world missionary meeting at Rochester some years ago, stretched out her hands to the audience in a pathetic appeal and said, "Sisters, we *must* have money for foreign missions"; and as she said it more than seven thousand dollars worth of diamonds flashed on her fingers; and yet we wonder why God does not answer our prayers. Oh, there is no wonder at all about it; the explanation is simple. It is found in the Word of God, it is because of our stinginess, our meanness, the smallness of our giving. Does not God say it in His Word, and is He not thundering it in our ears right now. *"Whoso stoppeth his ears at the cry of the poor,* he also shall cry himself, *but shall not be heard"*?

VI. *A Wrong Treatment of Husband or Wife*

There is one more hindrance to prayer which we must mention. We find it plainly stated in I Peter 3:7, "Likewise, ye husbands, dwell with your wives according to knowledge, giving honour unto the wife as unto the weaker vessel, and as being heirs together of the grace of life; *that your prayers be not hindered.*" That is plain enough, is it not? God here distinctly tells us that a wrong treatment of a wife by a husband (and vice versa, of course, a wrong treatment of a husband by a wife), hinders prayer; and it makes it impossible for God to hear the prayer of the husband or wife, as the case may be. Some of us are searching far and wide to discover what it is that hinders our prayer. We do not need to look so far away. Look into your home life. Husband, are you treating your wife as the Bible tells us a husband ought to treat his wife? Wives, are you treating your husbands as the Bible tells us wives ought to treat their husbands? If you are not, God will not hear your prayers. You may make all kinds of pretense of piety, you may be faithful in attending religious services and cooperating in Christian work, but God's eye is on your home life. The religion of our Lord Jesus Christ is a very *homely* religion. That is to say, it is a religion that enters right down into the practicalities of every day home life. That is one reason why I rejoice in it and am glad that I am a Christian. Christianity magnifies the home. Our modern modes of living, even among believers, "minifies" the home, but God doesn't.

How many a man there is in our churches today who, if you heard him talk in prayer-meeting, or in the missionary meeting, you would think he was a perfect saint of God; how soft and winning and earnest his words. And many a woman who hears him thinks, *How pleasant it must be to live with a husband like that.* But in his home he is quite different; he is cross, harsh, domineering, overbearing. He comes down to breakfast, and if by some mischance the bacon isn't cooked just right, perhaps it is a little burnt, he flies into a towering passion and he says to his wife, "Why can't we have a decent breakfast in this house? I buy the best and you are always burning it. If I can't get a good breakfast at home I am going to the hotel," and he rises from the table, hurries out of the room, takes his hat and starts for a restaurant; and his poor broken-hearted wife sits down and begins to sob. That man is actually shortening the life of his wife, and yet he wonders why God does not answer his prayers. Why, man, there is no wonder about it; it is because you are a brute, and God nowhere promises to answer the prayers of brutes—but of men, real 100 percent, Christian men.

I heard some years ago of a husband who did that very thing. He came to the breakfast table, the bacon was burned, he arose from the table cross and complaining, and stormed over the burnt bacon and said to his wife, "Why can't we have decent bacon in this house? If we can't I am going to the hotel." He dashed out of the room, took his hat and started for the hotel or somewhere else. His wife, of course, sank down by the table, buried her face in her arms and began to cry and sob. They had a darling little boy, a sweet sympathetic boy, and he stole up beside his sobbing mother and his arms stole around her neck, and he cried with her and he sobbed out, "Ma, I'm awfully sorry we married pa, ain't you?" And there is many a man today who so acts in his home, though he professes to be an earnest Christian, that he makes his children sorry that they "married pa," and yet he wonders why his prayers are not answered.

Take another illustration on the other side. How many a professedly Christian woman today is sweet as a summer morn, as winsome and alluring as a June breeze when she is at the missionary society, or the sewing circle, or any other public gathering of the church; but how different she is at home—cross, peevish, pettish, nagging. Her husband comes home tired from work. As they are about to sit down to the evening meal his wife says to him, "John, did you mail that letter I gave you this morning?"

He looks at her aghast, puts his hand in his pocket, and finds the letter there, and begins to apologize and says, "Wife, I am so sorry I forgot to mail it."

Then she storms, "Of course you forgot to mail it;

you always forget to mail it; you never do what I ask you to do," and thus she goes on and at last he, in anger and disgust, arises from the table, takes his hat and starts for his club. And that woman wonders how such a good Christian woman as she could have a drunkard for her husband. I'll tell you, woman, it is because you made him so. God forbid that I should justify a man in being a frequenter of places like that under any circumstances, but it is a simple matter of fact that many a man is a frequenter of clubs because his professedly Christian wife made his home so like hell that he felt he could not stay there. And yet that woman wonders why her prayers are not answered.

Take another illustration. How many a woman there is who a few years or even a few months ago, when a certain young man was coming around at night, stood before the glass and arrayed herself down to the smallest detail with the utmost care because "Charlie" was coming tonight. If it had been anyone else but Charlie she would not have taken such care, but it was Charlie. But now the months have passed and they have been married, perhaps several months. If anyone, any other gentleman, is coming home to dinner but her husband, she is as careful as ever to make herself look attractive; but "no one is coming tonight but Charlie," and any old dress is good enough, for "it is only Charlie." And yet she wonders why her prayers are not answered. Oh, men and women, if you and I are to expect God to answer our prayers we must take our Christianity into our home life, and we must be lovers always. I read a question some years ago in the *Ladies' Home Journal,* the question was, "How long should the honeymoon last?" I have forgotten what the answer given by the paper was, but I can tell you. Forever. Every year of married life should be more loving and tender and thoughtful than the one that went before, and it must be if we are to have power in prayer.

Men and women, if we are to have power in prayer we must look very carefully into our home life. And there are other things in married life that hinder prayer; other things that one cannot speak of in public, and yet how much they need to be spoken of in the day in which you and I are living. How many hideous abomi-

172

nations are covered up under the sacred name of marriage. Oh, men and women, if you and I are to have power in prayer we must spread our whole married life out before the all-seeing and all-searching and all-holy eye of God, and say to Him, "Heavenly Father, if there is anything in my married life anywhere that is displeasing in Thy sight, show me what it is and I will put it away." And then let us wait before God and let Him search our married life there in the white light of His Word, and the white light of the indwelling Spirit of God, and when He discloses any spot of any kind, as most likely He will, let us put it away. Then we shall have an open door of access to God, and our prayers will be no longer hindered but we will call to God and He will hear and give us what we seek from Him.

10

PREVAILING PRAYER AND REAL REVIVAL

"It is time for thee, Lord, to work; for they have made void thy law."—PSALM 119:126

Our subject is, Prevailing Prayer and Real Revival. I have five texts: please notice them very carefully.

You will find the first text in Psalm 119:126: *"It is time for thee,* LORD, *to work:* for they have made void thy law."

Our second text is Psalm 85:6: "Wilt thou not revive us again: that thy people may rejoice in thee?"

Our third text is Acts 1:14; 2:1-4, 41, 42: *"These* all *continued stedfastly* with one accord *in prayer and supplication* . . . And when the day of Pentecost was fully come, they were all with one accord in one place. *And suddenly there came a sound from heaven as of the rushing of a mighty wind,* and it *filled all the house* where they were sitting . . . And *they were all filled with the Holy Spirit,* and began to speak with other tongues, as the Spirit gave them utterance . . . Then they that gladly received his word were baptized: and *the same day there were added unto them about three thousand souls. And they continued stedfastly* in the apostles' doctrine and fellowship, and in breaking of bread, and in prayers."

Our fourth text is Ezekiel 37:9, 10: "Then said he unto me, Prophesy unto the wind, prophesy, son of man, and say to the wind, Thus saith the Lord GOD; *Come from the four winds, O breath, and breathe upon these slain, that they may live.* So I prophesied as He

174

commanded me, and the breath came into them, and they lived, and *stood up upon their feet, an exceeding great army."*

Our fifth text is Luke 11:13: "If ye then, being evil, know how to give good gifts unto your children: how much more shall your heavenly Father give the Holy Spirit to them that ask him?"

The great need of the church today is a general, widespread, deep, thoroughgoing, genuine revival. That is also the greatest need of business, the greatest need of human society, the greatest need of human government, the greatest need of international relations, the greatest need of missions. In every department of life today—business, social relations, politics, international relations, education, church—we are facing the most menacing problems and the most important crises that have confronted the human race in centuries, if not in human history, since the incarnation of God in the person of His Son Jesus Christ, and the birth of the church, which was the outcome of that incarnation. *The only hope* of the church is a great revival or revolution, revolution not only in Russia, but throughout the civilized world. It is a real and larger coming of the life of God into the church and through the church into society as a whole, or else it is universal Communism: Communism in church and state and school and home and everywhere, and consequent chaos and midnight darkness on the earth, and utter and universal dissolution and desolation and destruction.

Of course, those of us who know our Bibles at all well know that the final revival, the revival to be followed by no reaction but a revival resulting in a universal and permanent reign of righteousness on earth as well as in heaven, when God's kingdom will come and His will be done on earth as it is in heaven (Matt. 6:10), and when "the earth shall be full of the knowledge of the Lord, as the waters cover the sea" (Isa. 11:9), will only come as the result of the return of our Lord Jesus Christ to this earth to take the reins of government. The time of that coming is God's concern and not ours (Acts 1:7), and is in his hands, and for that coming we should pray (Rev. 22:20)and long intensely (II Pet.

175

3:12, R. V.) and wait; but that does not mean that we should in the meantime sit down and let things go to the dogs, and rather glory in the fact that things are getting worse and worse all the time, and congratulate ourselves on what fine folks we are and what a tough crowd the rest are in business and church and state. There is no Bible ground for being sure that the Lord may not tarry and that there may not be another revival, or, it may be, many revivals, before that glad day comes, and that most glorious of all revivals comes.

If Wesley had so reasoned in his day of widespread spiritual and theological darkness, or Martin Luther in his day, or John Knox in his day, or Jonathan Edwards in his day, or Charles G. Finney in his day, what would have become of the church, of the state, of human society and of the faith of God?

Whether the Lord Jesus comes soon or whether He tarries, we need a revival, and we need it badly, and if He should come within a year and find us doing our best to bring about that greatly needed revival, He would say to us, "Well done, thou good and faithful servant: thou hast been faithful over a few things, I will make thee ruler over many things: enter thou into the joy of thy Lord" (Matt. 25:21), and blessed will that servant be, "whom his Lord when he cometh shall find so doing" (Matt. 24:46). But if, on the other hand, He should come in this year and find us sitting in idle meditation on the glorious truth of His Second Coming and congratulating ourselves that we were "not as the rest of men are" (the men who "do not know the truth"), He would cut us asunder, and appoint us our portion with the rest of the hypocrites (Matt. 24:50, 51).

So my first prayer is, "Even so, come, Lord Jesus" (Rev. 22:20). But as I do not know and cannot know how soon that prayer will be answered (as God has seen fit to "set" the times and seasons "within his own authority"—Acts 1:7), my second prayer is, and it is getting to be a more and more intense and insistent prayer, "Lord, send a revival," and (as far as I am concerned) "let it begin in me."

What I have to say will come under three heads:

176

First, what a real revival is, and what the results of a real revival are.

Second, the need of a real revival.

Third, the relation of persistent prayer to a real revival.

I. What a Real Revival Is

First, then, let us consider what a real revival is and what its results are.

1. *A real revival is a time of quickening or impartation of life.* That is exactly what the word "revival" means according to its etymology, and, also, according to its usage today, and that is exactly what the Hebrew word translated "revive" in our second text, "Wilt thou not revive us again" (Psa. 85:6) means, and it is so translated in the Revised Version, "Wilt thou not *quicken* us (i. e., impart life to us) again." As God alone can give life, *a revival is a time when God visits His people, and, by the power of His Spirit, imparts new life to them, and through them imparts life to sinners dead in trespasses and sins.* We frequently have religious excitements and enthusiasms aroused by the cunning methods and hypnotic influence of the mere professional evangelist or "revivalist," but these are not revivals, and are not needed: they are a curse and not a blessing; they are the devil's imitations of a revival. *New life from God*—that is a revival. A general revival is a time when this new life from God is not confined to scattered localities, but is general throughout Christendom and the earth.

The reason why a general revival is needed is that spiritual dearth and desolation and death is general. It is not confined to any one country, though it may be more manifest in some countries than in others. It is found in our foreign mission fields as well as in our home fields. We have had, and are having, local revivals. The life-giving Spirit of God has breathed upon this minister and that, this church and that, this community and that; but what we need, and sorely need, is a revival that shall be widespread and general.

2. Now, in order that we may have a more complete

idea of what a revival really is, let us look at the results of a revival.

(1) The first results are in ministers of the Gospel.

a. *In times of revival the minister has a new love for souls.* We ministers, as a rule, have no such love for souls as we ought to have, no such love for souls as our Lord Jesus had, no such love for souls as Paul had. But when God visits His people, the hearts of ministers are greatly burdened for the unsaved: they go out in great longing for the salvation of their fellow-men; they forget their ambition to preach great sermons, and their ambitions for fame; they long for one thing, and one thing only: to see men brought to Christ and thus saved.

b. *When true revivals come, ministers get a new love for God's Word and a new faith in God's Word.* They fling to the winds their doubts and their criticisms of the Bible and of the creeds, and go to preaching the Bible, and, especially, Christ crucified. *Revivals make ministers who are loose in their doctrines orthodox. A* genuine, wide-sweeping revival would do more to get our ministers and theological professors right in their doctrine than all the heresy trials that were ever instituted.

c. *Revivals bring to ministers new liberty, new joy and new power in preaching.* It is no week-long grind to prepare a sermon, and no nerve-consuming effort to preach it after it has been prepared. Preaching becomes a joy and a refreshment, and there is real power in it in times of revival.

(2) Now, let us look at the results of a revival in Christians generally. The results of a revival in Christians generally are as marked as its results upon the ministry.

a. *In times of revival, Christians come out from the world and live separated lives.* Christians who have been dallying with the world, who have been playing cards and dancing and going to the theatres and the movies, and indulging in similar unbecoming follies, give them up. They get a new spiritual vision, by which they see clearly that these things are incompatible with their increasing life and light.

b. *In times of revival, Christians get a new spirit of prayer.* Prayer-meetings are no longer a mere duty, but

178

become the necessity of a hungry, importunate heart. Private prayer is followed with new zest. The voice of earnest prayer to God is heard day and night. People no longer ask, "Does God answer prayer?"; they know He does, and besiege the throne of grace day and night.

c. *In times of revival, Christians go to work for lost souls.* They do not go to meetings simply to enjoy themselves and get blest. They go to meetings to watch for souls and bring them to Christ. They talk to men on the street and in the stores and in their homes. The cross of Christ, salvation, heaven and hell become the subjects of constant conversation. Politics and the weather and Easter bonnets and the latest novels are forgotten. The things of God occupy the whole horizon of their thought.

d. *In times of revival, Christians have new joy in the Lord Jesus* (Acts 2:46; John 15:11). Life is always joy, and new life is new joy. Revival days are glad days, exceedingly glad days, "days of heaven on earth" (Deut. 11:21).

e. *In times of revival, Christians get a new love for the Word of God:* they want to study it day and night. Revivals are bad for saloons and clubs and parties and theatres and movies, but they are good for book stores and Bible agencies.

(3) Now let us look at the results of real revival on the unsaved world. Revivals have a most decided influence on the unsaved world.

a. First of all, *real revivals bring a deep conviction of sin.* Our Lord said that when the Spirit was come, He would "convict the world of sin" (John 16:7, 8). Now, we have seen that a revival is a coming of the Holy Spirit, and therefore there must be a new conviction of sin, and there always is. If you see something that men call a revival and there is no conviction of sin, you may know at once that it is not a real revival, but a bogus revival. This is a sure mark of real revival: deep conviction of sin.

b. *Real revivals also bring conversions and regenerations.* When God refreshes His people, He always converts sinners also. The first result of Pentecost was new life and power to the 120 disciples in the upper room; the second result was 3,000 conversions in a

179

single day. It is always so. I am constantly reading of revivals here and there, where Christians were greatly helped, but where there were no conversions. I have my doubts about all such revivals. If Christians are truly refreshed, they will get after the unsaved by prayer and testimony and persuasion and preaching and personal work, and there will be, there must be, conversions, real conversions, regenerated lives, lives completely transformed: infidels becoming earnest believers in Jesus Christ; drunkards becoming sober; impure men and women becoming pure; thieves becoming honest men and industrious citizens; and lazy people getting down gladly to hard work. A true revival always begins in the hearts of those who are already Christians, but it never ends there. It goes out to the unsaved and there are definite conversions.

II. *The Need of Revival*

Now let us look at the need of a revival at the present time.

I think that the mere description of what a revival is and what a revival does, shows that it is needed, sorely needed, but let us look at some specific conditions that exist today that show the need of a revival. If one dwells upon these conditions he is likely to be called a pessimist. If facing the facts is to be called a pessimist, I am willing to be called a pessimist. I am in actual fact an optimist, an optimist of the optimists; but I am not a blind optimist, i. e., one who is an optimist by shutting his eyes to facts that are as clear as day. If to be an optimist, one must shut his eyes and call black white and error truth and sin righteousness and death life, I have no desire to be an optimist; but I am an optimist all the same. Pointing out the real conditions which are very bad will lead to better conditions.

1. Look first at the ministry:

(1) *Many of us who are professedly orthodox ministers are practically infidels.* That may be pretty plain speech, but it is also indisputable fact. There is no essential difference between the teachings of Tom Paine and Bob Ingersoll, on the one hand, and the teachings of some of our theological professors on the other.

180

Theological professors are not so blunt and honest about it as Tom Paine and Bob Ingersoll were, they phrase it in more elegant and studied and honied sentences; but their teaching means the same thing and produces the same damnable results. Much of the so-called "New Learning" and "Higher Criticism" and "Modernism" is simply Tom Paine infidelity sugar-coated and flavored with a pretense of piety. A number of years ago, Prof. Howard Osgood, who was a real scholar and not a mere huckster of German infidelity, once read a statement of some positions held by the modernists of his day, who were not essentially different from the modernists of today, though not quite so bad, and he then asked if these positions as he read them did not fairly represent the scholarly criticism of the day, and the critics themselves admitted that they did; just then he threw a bomb into the ranks of the "Higher Critics" by saying, "I am reading verbatim from Tom Paine's *Age of Reason*."

There is little new in "The Higher Criticism," or in modernistic or liberal theology in general. Our future ministers oftentimes are being educated under infidel professors, and being, when they enter the college of theological seminary, really only immature boys, they naturally come out infidels in many cases, and then go forth to poison the church.

(2) *Even when our ministers are orthodox,* as, thank God, so large a number are today, *nevertheless oftentimes they are not men of prayer.* How many modern ministers, do you suppose, know what it means to "agonize in prayer" (Rom 15:30, Greek) and to wrestle in prayer, to spend a good share of a night in prayer? Of course, we do not know how many, but I do know that many do not.

(3) *Many of us who are ministers have no love for souls.* How many of us preach because we *must* preach, preach because we feel that men everywhere are perishing, and by our preaching hope to save some? How many of us follow up our preaching as Paul did his, by "beseeching men everywhere" to be reconciled to God? (II Cor. 5:20; Acts 20:31).

Perhaps we have said enough about ministers, but it is evident that a revival is needed for our sake, or some of us will have to stand before God overwhelmed with confusion in that awful day of reckoning that is surely coming (Rom. 14:12).

2. Let us now look at the church:

(1) *Look at the doctrinal state of the church today. It is surely bad enough, and apparently getting worse all the time.* Many of our church members do not believe in the whole Bible. To many, the book of Genesis is a myth, Jonah is an allegory, and even the miracles of the Son of God are questioned. They have been denied in a recent article in one of our most popular and widely circulated magazines by one of the most prominent Presbyterian ministers in this country, a member of the Board of Foreign Missions of the Presbyterian Church. With a great many, the doctrine of prayer is old-fashioned, and the work of the Holy Spirit is sneered at. We are told that conversion and regeneration are unnecessary, and hell is no longer believed in. Then look at the fads and errors that have sprung up in consequence of this loss of faith and creedal chaos: Christian Science, Unitarianism, Spiritualism, Universalism, Pastor Russellism, Babism, Theosophy, Metaphysical Healing, and a perfect pandemonium of "doctrines of devils."

(2) *Look at the spiritual state of the church.*

a. *Worldliness is rampant, if not regnant, among church members.* Many church members are just as eager as any in the rush to get rich. They use the methods of the world in the accumulation of wealth, and they hold on to it just as tightly as any worldling when they get it.

b. *Prayerlessness abounds among church members on every hand.* It is doubtful if one in ten of the church members of this country attend the prayer-meeting with any regularity, and secret prayer takes little of the time or attention of the average church member. Someone has said that Christians, on an average, do not spend more than five minutes a day in secret prayer. Of course, none of us know whether that is true or not, but I fear that it is far truer than most of us suspect.

c. *Neglect of the Word of God goes hand in hand with neglect of prayer to God.* Many professed Christians spend twice as much time every day of their lives in wallowing through the mire of the daily papers as they do bathing in the cleansing laver of God's Holy Word. How many Christians average an hour a day spent in Bible study?

d. *Along with neglect of prayer and neglect of the Word of God goes a lack of generosity.* The churches are rapidly increasing in wealth, but the treasuries of the missionary societies are empty. Evangelical church members do not average more than a few dollars a year for foreign missions. It is simply appalling.

e. Then, *there is an increasing disregard for the Lord's Day.* "The First Day of the Week" has largely become a day of worldly pleasure, instead of a day of holy service. The Sunday newspaper, with its inane twaddle and filthy scandal, takes the place of the Sunday school and church service.

f. *Church members mingle with the world in all forms of questionable amusements.* In many places, the young man or young woman who does not believe in the dance, with its rank immodesties, the card table, with its strong drift toward gambling, and the theatre and the movies, with their increasing appeal to lewdness, is counted an old fogy, a relic of a played-out Puritanism.

Then, what a small proportion of our membership has really entered into fellowship with Jesus Christ, with His burden of souls. But enough has been said of the spiritual state of the church.

3. Now, look at the state of the world:

(1) Note, first of all, *how few conversions there are.* Many churches last year lost more members than they gained. Here and there a church has a large number of accessions upon confession of faith, but these churches are rare exceptions; and even where there are many *accessions,* in how few cases are *the conversions deep, thorough and satisfactory.*

(2) There is also, in most circles, *an utter lack of deep conviction of sin;* seldom are men overwhelmed with a sense of their awful guilt in trampling under foot the Son of God. Sin is regarded as a mere "misfortune," or as "infirmity," or even as "good in the making"; seldom is it regarded as an enormous wrong against a holy God, deserving of eternal damnation.

(3) *Unbelief is rampant.* Many regard it as a mark of intellectual superiority to reject the Bible, and even faith in a personal God and a future life. In most cases they are all the more proud of this mark of intellectual superiority because it is the only mark of intellectual superiority that they possess.

(4) *Hand in hand with this wide-spread infidelity goes the grossest immorality,* as has always been the case. Infidelity and immorality are Siamese twins: they always exist and always grow and always fatten together. This prevailing immorality is found everywhere. *Look at the legalized adultery that we call divorce.* Much so-called marriage is little more than legalized prostitution. Men marry one wife and then another, and are still admitted into good society, and women do likewise. There are thousands of supposedly respectable men in America living with other men's wives, and thousands of supposedly respectable women living with other women's husbands.

The increasing immorality is seen in the state of the theatre. The theatre, at its best, is bad enough, but now plays reeking with evil suggestion seem to rule the day, and the women who debauch themselves by appearing in such plays are defended in the newspapers and welcomed by supposedly respectable people. The movies are even viler than the theatre ever dared to be, and the rottenness of them is paraded before our eyes in the newspapers that we are urged to receive into our homes and let our children read.

Much of our literature is rotten, but people will read books that a few years ago would have been in danger of bringing their publishers under the ban of the law against obscene literature; I say even supposedly decent people read these books because they are the rage.

Art is frequently a mere covering for shameless indecency. Women are induced to cast all modesty and decency to the winds that the artist may perfect his art and defile his morals by employing them as "models."

Greed for money has become a mania with both rich and poor. The multi-millionaire will often sell his soul and trample the rights of his fellow-men under foot in the mad hope of becoming a billionaire, and the laboring man will often commit murder to increase the pow-

184

er of the union and to keep up wages. *Wars are waged and men shot down like dogs and gassed and subjected to all kinds of cruelty to improve commerce and to gain political prestige for unprincipled politicians who parade as statesmen.*

The wild and almost incredible licentiousness of the day lifts its serpent head everywhere. You see it in the newspapers, you see it on the billboards, you see it in the advertisements. You see it on the streets at night. You see it just outside the church door. You find it not only in the awful cesspools set apart for it in the great cities, but it is crowding into our hotels and apartment houses and into the residential portions of our cities. Alas! now and then you find it, if you look sharply, in supposedly respectable homes, indeed it will be borne to your ears by the confessions of broken-hearted men and women. *The moral condition of the world in our day is disgusting, reeking, sickening, appalling.*

We need a revival, deep, widespread, general, in the power of the Holy Ghost. It is either a general revival or a general dissolution of the church, the home and the state. A revival, new life from God, is the cure, and the only cure, that will stem the awful tide of immorality and unbelief. Mere argument will not do it, but a wind from heaven, a new outpouring of the Holy Ghost, a true, God-sent revival will. Infidelity, higher criticism, liberalism, modernism, Christian Science, spiritualism, universalism, theosophy, all will go down before the outpouring of the Spirit of God. It was not discussion and argument and reasoning, but the breath of God that relegated Tom Paine, Voltaire, Volney, and the other triumphant infidels of old to the limbo of forgetfulness; and we need a new breath from God to send the German destructive critics of our day, and the parrots that they have trained to occupy university chairs and evangelical pulpits in England and America, to keep them company.

III. *The Place of Prayer in Revival.*

We now come to the place of prayer in revival. This is the most important point I have to make, and all that I have said thus far is simply a preparation for this and was intended to lead up to this. But what needs to be said can be said in a few words.

The great need of today, as we have said, is a general revival; that is clear and admits of no honest difference of opinion. *What, then, shall we do? Pray.* Take up the Psalmist's prayer, "Wilt thou not revive us again: that thy people may rejoice in thee?" Take up Ezekiel's prayer, "Come from the four winds, O breath (i. e., breath of God), and breathe upon these slain, that they may live."

The first great revival of Christian history had its origin, on the human side, in a ten days' prayer-meeting. We read of that handful of disciples, "These all *continued stedfastly with one accord in prayer and supplication.*" The result of that prayer-meeting we read in the next chapter of the Acts of the Apostles, "They were all filled with the Holy Ghost, and began to speak with other tongues, as the Spirit gave them utterance" (Acts 2:4). Further on in the same chapter we read, "And the same day there were added unto them about three thousand souls" (Acts 2:41), and in the next verse we read how real and lasting the revival proved, for these are the words there recorded, "And they continued stedfastly in the apostles' doctrine and fellowship, and in breaking of bread, and in prayers," and in the last verse of the chapter we read, "And the Lord added to the church daily those that were being saved."

The great revival in Acts 4 came in the same way. A time of great peril had come to the church, that seemed to threaten its very existence. The two great leaders of the church, Peter and John, had been arrested, imprisoned and threatened with death. What did the church do? We read, "And being let go, they went to their own company, and reported all that the chief priests and elders had said unto them. And when they heard that, *they lifted up their voice to God with one accord*" (Acts 4:23, 24). Further on we read, "And when they had prayed, the place was shaken where they were assembled together; and they were all filled with the Holy Ghost, and they spake the Word of God with boldness. And the multitude of them that believed were of one heart and of one soul: neither said any of them that ought of the things which he possessed was

186

his own; but they had all things common. And with great power gave the apostles their witness of the resurrection of the Lord Jesus: and great grace was upon them all. Neither was there any among them that lacked: for as many as were possessors of lands or houses sold them, and brought the prices of the things that were sold, And laid them down at the apostles' feet: and distribution was made unto every man according as he had need" (Acts 4:31-35).

Every true revival from that day to this has had its earthly origin in prayer. "The Great Awakening" under Jonathan Edwards in the eighteenth century began with his famous call to prayer, and he carried it forward by prayer. It has been recorded of Jonathan Edwards that he "so labored in prayer that he wore the hard wooden boards into grooves where his knees pressed so often and so long."

The marvelous work of grace among the North American Indians under David Brainerd, Jonathan Edwards' son-in-law, in 1743 and the following years, had its origin in the days and nights that Brainerd spent before God in prayer for an enduement of power from on high for this work.

But we can go further back than that, and see how a revival is always the result of prayer. In the early part of the seventeenth century there was a great religious awakening in Ulster, Ireland. The lands of the rebel chiefs, which had been forfeited to the British crown, were settled up by a class of colonists who for the most part were governed by a spirit of wild adventure. Real piety was rare. Seven ministers, five from Scotland and two from England, settled in that country, the earliest arrivals coming in 1613. Of one of these ministers, named Blair, it is recorded by a contemporary, "He spent many days and nights in prayer, alone and with others, and was vouchsafed great intimacy with God." Mr. James Glendenning, a man of meager natural gifts, was also a man of prayer. The work began under this man Glendenning. The historian of the times, "He was a man who never would have been chosen by a wise assembly of ministers, nor sent to begin a reformation in this land. Yet this was the Lord's choice to begin with him the admirable work of God which I mention on purpose that all may see how the glory is only the Lord's in making a holy nation in this profane land, and that it was 'not by might, nor by power, nor by man's wisdom, but by my Spirit, saith the Lord.'" By James Glendenning's preaching at Oldstone multitudes of hearers felt in great anxiety and terror of conscience. They looked upon themselves as altogether lost and damned, and cried out, "Men and brethren, what shall we do to be saved?" They were stricken into a swoon by the power of His Word. A dozen in one day were carried out of doors as dead. These were not women, but some of the boldest spirits of the neighborhood, "some who had formerly feared not with their swords to put a whole market town into a fray." Concerning one of them, the historian writes, "I have heard one of them, then a mighty strong man, now a mighty Christian, say that his end in coming into church was to consult with his companions how to work some mischief."

This work spread throughout the whole country. By the year 1626 a monthly concert of prayer was held in Antrim. The work spread beyond the bounds of Down and Antrim to the churches of the neighboring counties. So great became the religious interest that Christians would come thirty or forty miles to the communions, and continue from the time they came until they returned without wearying or making use of sleep. Many of them neither ate nor drank, and yet some of them professed that they "went away most fresh and vigorous, their souls so filled with the sense of God." This revival changed the whole character of northern Ireland.

I have told you in other chapters of the great revival, the marvelous work of God, in Ulster and other northern counties of Ireland in 1859 and 1860: that, too, came by prayer. About the spring of 1858 a work of power began to manifest itself. It spread from town to town and from county to county. The congregations became too large for the buildings, and the meetings were held in the open air, often attended by many thousands of people. Many hundreds of persons were frequently convicted of sin in a single meeting. In some places the criminal courts and jails were closed for lack

188

of occupation. There were manifestations of the Holy Spirit's convicting and regenerating power of a most remarkable character, clearly proving that the Holy Spirit is as ready to work today as in apostolic days, when ministers and Christians really believe in Him and begin to prepare the way by prayer for Him to work.

It was in answer to the prayers of Wesley and his associates that the Lord saved the church and the state in England in the early part of the eighteenth century. The little group met for prayer long before God so wonderfully used them in preaching, and even a historian so utterly rationalistic as Lecky admits that it was the Wesleyan Revival that saved England politically and commercially and every other way. Conditions were appalling when the group of believers whom God had aroused and endued with the spirit of supplication began to pray. One observer remarks of the English of that day that they were "the most lifeless in Europe." It is said that "the greater part of the prominent statesmen of that time were unbelievers in any form of Christianity, and distinguished for the grossness and immorality of their lives," and yet in answer to the prayers of a company of godly men, the prayers that would not take no for an answer, there came such a religious revival that in a few years the whole character of English society was changed, and there came a period of great spiritual life and activity in the church.

The wonderful revival of 1857 and 1858 in this country, which has been described as "the greatest revival known since the days of the apostles," was the result of prayer: first, the prayers of an obscure city missionary in New York, and then the prayers of those that he succeeded in associating with him in his burden of a desire for a revival. It has been said of America at the time immediately preceding this revival, that its moral and spiritual degradation was such that "the whole country was on the very verge of a volcanic eruption of vice and political disaster"; but prayer prevailed with God, the spirit of prayer spread, prayer-meetings were held in New York in churches and theatres, attended by thousands: prayer-meetings were held every hour of the day and night, and a chain of prayer

189

was formed of 2,000 miles in length, and there was such an outpouring of the Spirit of God that countless thousands were born again, and the influence of that great work crossed the Atlantic Ocean and led to the prayers in the north of Ireland that resulted in the great Ulster Revival of which we have spoken in an earlier chapter.

The great awakening under Mr. Moody in England, Scotland and Ireland and America, and the results of which were felt in all the missionary countries of the earth and in the distant islands of the sea, had its origin, on the manward side, in prayer. Mr. Moody, though from the time of his conversion a most active worker, made no real impression until men and women began to cry to God. His going to England at all was in answer to the importunate cries of a bed-ridden saint, and while the spirit of prayer continued, that wonderful work of God abode in strength, but in the course of time less and less was made of prayer, and the work of that mighty man of God fell off very perceptibly in power.

Beyond a doubt, one of the great secrets of the unsatisfactoriness and superficiality and unreality and temporary character of many of our modern, so-called revivals is that so much dependence is put upon man's machinery and so little upon God's power, sought and obtained by the earnest, persistent, believing prayer that will not take no for an answer. We live in a day characterized by the multiplication of man's machinery and the diminution of God's power. The great cry of our day is work, work, work, organize, organize, organize, give us some new society, tell us some new methods, devise some new machinery; *but the great need of our day is prayer, more prayer and better prayer.*

Prayer could work as marvelous results today as it ever could, if the church would only betake itself to praying, real praying, prevailing prayer. There seem to be increasing signs that the church is awakening to that fact. Here and there God is laying upon individual ministers and churches a burden of prayer that they have never known before. Many are getting entirely disgusted with mere machinery and with man-made revivals, and are learning to depend more upon God.

190

Ministers are crying to God day and night for power. In a few places, perhaps many, churches or portions of churches are meeting together in the early morning hours and the late evening hours crying to God for abundant rain. There are indications of the coming of a mighty and widespread revival.

What is needed is a general revival, but if we cannot have a general revival, sweeping over the whole earth, we can have local revivals and state revivals and national revivals. It is not necessary that the whole church get to praying to begin with. Great revivals always begin first in the hearts of a few men and women whom God arouses by His Spirit to believe in Him as a living God, as a God who answers prayer, and upon whose heart He lays a burden from which no rest can be found except in importunate crying unto God. Oh, may He, by His Spirit, lay such a burden upon our hearts today. I believe He will.